GIVING MUCH/GAINING MORE

Giving Much/
Gaining More

Mentoring for Success

Emily M. Wadsworth

Purdue University Press
West Lafayette, Indiana

Printed in the United States of America

Library of Congress Cataloging-in-Publication Data

Wadsworth, Emily M., 1934–
Giving much/gaining more / Emily M. Wadsworth.
p.   cm.
ISBN 1-55753-291-5
1. Engineering—vocational guidance. 2. Mentoring in the
professions—Case studies. 3. Women engineers—Vocational
guidance. I. Title.
TA157 .w28 2002
620' .0023—dc21

2002006205

Proceeds from book sales will underwrite annual mentoring awards
given to female engineering students at Purdue University.

This book is lovingly dedicated to
my husband, Hank,
our sons, Frank, Robert, and Richard,
and written in memory of
our daughter, Mary

Contents

Acknowledgments

Gratitude goes to the following people for sharing their expertise, time, and suggestions:

Editor
  Tim Wallace

Advisors
  Margaret Trimmer
  Carol Dunn

Readers
  Lyn Doyle
  Larry Huggins
  Donna Keenan
  Boyd Keenan
  Martha Kramer
  Mary Ann Oyer

Graphic Designers
  Michael Kelsey
  Dan Kirchmann

Supporters of Mentoring Programs
  Ted Greenwood, Program Director,
  Alfred P. Sloan Foundation

  Deans, School and Department Heads, Faculty, and Directors in the Schools of Engineering, Purdue University

Reflections: A Dream Fulfilled

As a 12-year-old girl growing up in Greece, I watched with millions of others around the globe as Purdue alumnus Neil Armstrong made his "giant leap for mankind," the historic moon landing captured on video clips from NASA's launch control room in Houston and delivered to my home through television. I was struck by the images I saw, and it was then that I decided to become an electronics engineer. My dream was to work for NASA.

I enrolled in the National Technical University in Greece in 1972 to study electrical engineering, with the support of my family. At the university, I was one of three women in a group of 150 students. The undergraduate experience was difficult, primarily because I felt lonely and isolated. I heard explicit remarks that I probably wasn't going to make it through to the end.

I did graduate in engineering and went on to complete masters and doctoral degrees at UCLA in the United States. I joined the faculty of the University of Michigan and wound up working for a NASA-funded university center. My research in microwave circuitry, with applications to wireless communications systems, radars, and receivers for deep-space communications, has brought great satisfaction. My dream has been realized.

My titles and responsibilities have changed over the course of my career, culminating now with my appointment as Dean of Engineering at Purdue. Among the many initiatives that we in the Schools of Engineering are taking up—forming our strategic plan, executing a comprehensive building program, establishing high-impact research centers—stands one cross-cutting, strategic initiative that I consider crucial: dramatically increasing the number of women and underrepresented minorities who earn engineering degrees from our university and who populate our faculty.

Mentoring programs like those developed by Dr. Emily Wadsworth at Purdue have proved invaluable to creating that supportive climate, that feeling of belonging, which so often makes the difference in students' success. The reflections of the young women who contributed to this book make clear that healthy mentoring relationships not only boost those statistics that we educators particularly care about—students' academic performance and their retention rates—but also, inevitably, spur program participants toward personal growth and maturity.

As I read these pages of *Giving Much/Gaining More*, inspired as I was to pursue engineering because of a Purdue alumnus, I am impressed by the insights, strength, resilience, and persistence of these more recently minted alumnae—and gratified that at Purdue, through joyous times and painful setbacks, they found a setting in which they could learn to thrive. "We don't receive wisdom," wrote the novelist Marcel Proust. "We must discover it for ourselves after a journey that no one can take for us or spare us."

—LINDA P. B. KATEHI
John A. Edwardson Dean of Engineering
Purdue University

Foreword

This unique book on the perspectives of those in a highly successful mentoring program for women exemplifies important new directions for formal mentoring practice. With its origins in Greek mythology, mentoring has long been an informal practice in which a seasoned person groomed a less experienced person (both usually were men) to succeed in a system such as a corporation. This informal mentoring helped ensure stability within a business or other organization and is called "grooming mentoring." Unfortunately, grooming of selected individuals did little to promote diversity or to stimulate change within the organization.

In the 1970s, heightened interest in mentoring was spurred by a landmark study of 40 white, upper middle class males, which was reported in *The Seasons of a Man's Life* by Daniel Levinson and his colleagues. The authors effectively portrayed the positive difference mentoring could make in a man's career. The interest in mentoring stimulated by this popular book kindled enthusiasm for utilizing mentoring to promote success for underrepresented people, as well. This was especially true of academic and corporate settings that were actively seeking diversity and renewal.

Thus, formal mentoring programs for women and minorities became *de rigeur* in forward-looking organizations in the past two decades. At first, however, such programs sought to formalize grooming mentoring, i.e., matching mentors with protégées (or mentees) on the basis of similarities, emphasizing the contributions to be made by a powerful mentor to her protégée's success, and promoting mentoring practices that would allow protégées to fit into existing organizations by adopting the thought and actions of those who have succeeded in the past. In these programs, then, well-intentioned people focused on practical aspects of bringing newcomers into organizations and helping them be as much like the incumbents as possible.

In the mid-1980s, this approach was enhanced by a new mentoring concept—networking mentoring—which was described by Marion Swoboda and Susan Millar. Based upon their experiences working with women administrators in Minnesota institutions of higher education, they presented this mentoring alternative, which has been well-received by underrepresented people and by dynamic organizations.

Networking mentoring is characterized by connecting individuals as an organized group with facilitation by those who are more experienced. It emphasizes a productive exchange through which individuals learn from and give to others in the group by sharing information, encouraging, supporting, coaching, sponsoring, and role modeling. Finally, networking mentoring values the enrichment inherent in diversity. This support of diversity leads to empowerment of individuals in the network who then contribute their perspectives to change institutions, whether the individuals are students or employees.

Thus the stage was set in 1992 when I facilitated a doctoral-level seminar on my area of scholarship and professional practice— mentoring. The talented individuals who participated in this semester-long experience examined developmental theory, mentoring concepts and models (grooming mentoring and networking mentoring), and research on mentoring practice. All focused on utilizing the seminar to strengthen ongoing or proposed mentoring programs to which they were committed. Dr. Emily Wadsworth, who audited the seminar, was dedicated to the Mentor and Mentee (M&M) Programs described in this book. She was highly committed to designing and implementing high-quality, accountable, networking mentoring programs for Women in Engineering that would be assured of success. And succeed she did!

Throughout the past decade, it has been my pleasure to interact with the M&M programs by presenting orientations on mentoring roles, responsibilities, and research to program participants. I also have cited these programs as exemplars of accountability. In fact, the M&M programs have been a stunning success, as readers will glean from the chapters in this book. It is a tribute to the M&M founder, Emy Wadsworth, and to the many students who have formed the program's networks that the application of mentoring theory has resulted in resoundingly meaningful programs. Their gifts to each other have been many; and now they share their bounty with all who read this book.

—Marilyn J. Haring
Former Dean, School of Education
Purdue University

GIVING MUCH/GAINING MORE

Introduction

Two major turning points in my life were a near death experience in 1967 when I was 33 years old and the death of our only daughter, Mary, in 1990 when she was 32 years old. The first started me on a personal journey, an inner struggle to discover who I was meant to be and what I was meant to do. The second, while extremely personal, propelled me further in a professional career, an area where I could relay my life experiences to others.

This book, unknowingly by me, had its beginning in 1990 when I was asked to conduct a national survey of Women in Engineering Programs [WIEP] at degree granting engineering institutions throughout the United States. A summary of the results revealed that a major concern of the 293 schools surveyed was recruitment and retention of female students in engineering. I collected information on WIEP at 186 of these schools, including enrollments of female versus male students, scope and content of program activities, and number of degrees for females versus males. Summarizing these data and reading literature on university programs gave me an understanding of the broad array of existing recruitment and retention activities and their outcomes. Two points were evident: 1] the

critical time for retention of students was during the first year; and 2]
women students transfer out of engineering due to feelings of isolation and incompetence. To effectively counter these trends, programs were needed where females had role models, were regularly
supported by peers, had their self-esteem affirmed, received pertinent strategies, and were encouraged to persist.

The following year, I became an administrator for Women in
Engineering Programs at Purdue University and was challenged to
create a set of mentoring programs, under a grant from the Alfred P.
Sloan Foundation, which would retain female engineering students.
Mentoring is defined as significant personal and professional assistance given by a more experienced person to a less experienced person during a time of transition. Personal assistance involved role
modeling and encouraging while professional assistance included
educating and sponsoring. In order to accomplish these tasks, I
reflected on my own life, about whom and what had influenced me
during my collegiate years. My siblings held great importance; they
provided me with acceptance, care, compassion, and counseling.
Particularly relevant was the invaluable support and guidance given
by my next older sister and her friends throughout my first two
years as an undergraduate. I now envisioned that a similar set of mutually reinforcing actions might help female students to remain in
engineering.

My initial effort to increase retention was to bring together small
teams of students to act as staff members who would prepare,
present, and assess a set of mentoring programs that were given the
initials M&M for Mentees and Mentors. Two teams, each with four
people, would lead the Undergraduate Mentoring Programs while
one team of five people would lead the Graduate Mentoring Program. These programs each involved about fifty people a year: third
year junior students coaching first year students during their initial

start in college; fourth year seniors encouraging second year students as they became involved in specific engineering majors; and Ph.D. students sponsoring M.S. students as they moved through their graduate programs. I met regularly with these three teams throughout the academic year.

During weekly sessions, monthly meetings, and social times in my home, team members, an administrative assistant, and I together formed a unity of purpose. We pooled our individual skills to identify and resolve problem situations raised by students. We established ground rules, rotated designated roles, and evaluated program events. Week by week, as the programs matured and we all got to know each other better, team members would ask me questions about human behaviors and relationships. They wanted to know the source of my ideas and feelings. They asked me to explain how I had caught actions in the first three decades of my personal life and how I had cast actions over three decades of my professional career. They really wanted to know whether or not I currently used what I was talking about with my husband and immediate family.

Through sharing insights, my values were becoming clear to team members. For example, they found I believed that by coming together as a staff unit, individuals could effectively unite their talents. The combined competencies could be greater than the simple sum of each person acting on their own. I also was convinced that within a group's aura, the attributes of each individual could grow faster and linger longer than if each person existed on their own.

Team members discovered that I thought simple actions like welcoming and excluding could have profound results. Together, we discussed standards of conduct that could influence student retention. For example, did treating people with respect and as persons of worth make a difference in their attitudes towards fellow peers and classroom assignments? Our collective goal as staff members was to progress from using debilitating actions like doubting and ridiculing and move towards using enabling actions like trusting and affirming. Working together in this manner led us away from unproductive outcomes such as feelings of insecurity and suppression and propelled us towards productive outcomes such as greater personal confidence and openness. The synergy of these team members effectively set the mentoring programs up for success and sustained individuals through the best and worst of times.

The results from a four-year study were that retention rates dramatically increased for female undergraduate engineering students who participated in our mentoring programs. Also, over three years, proportions of females receiving graduate degrees in engineering were consistently higher for graduate students participating in our mentoring program than for those not participating. Finally, unanticipated benefits for team members were that times spent staffing the mentoring programs helped them further develop their leadership skills, better refine their oral and written communication, and expand their social and professional networks. After graduation, individual members became competent professionals and able leaders of project teams in their respective corporations, laboratories, and organizations. They are currently mentoring other men and women throughout the world.

Personal outcomes included close cross-generational relationships between students and me. Often I would say, "You were accepted in engineering at Purdue, you can make it in engineering at Purdue." They have proven me right when I told them they could persist against all odds, graduate with degrees, and move on to assist others wherever they might be. After team members left the university, we continued to have numerous communications via email messages, cards, and a Summer Serendipities Newsletter. I have attended their showers, weddings, and received birth announcements for their children. When members have returned to Purdue, they have visited me. It is they who have urged me to write this book.

While collaborating on this project with former students, a decision was made to rediscover and refine many of our past experiences in order to focus on our present lives and future possibilities. During this process we thought of some opposing actions, polarities, that might exist together in everyone and which push and pull us in different directions. Twelve pairs came to mind:

welcoming & excluding
communicating & bickering
trusting & doubting
accepting & rejecting
affirming & ridiculing
forgiving & condemning
reframing & stagnating
letting go & holding tight
rejoicing & grieving
balancing & tilting
focusing & blurring
gracing & alienating

These actions began in our formative years and came about as a result of different ways in which we were raised and various environments in which we lived. Since polarities are contradictory, they create tensions and frustrations when we are required to make decisions. Until we recognize these opposing forces for what they are, we might have trouble harnessing our energy and emotions in a constructive way. This difficulty can lead to problems when we consider later the consequences of what decisions we might have made.

This book is focused on the above polarities. Each chapter includes my meanings for a pair of actions. Then there is the story of how I caught these actions in my personal life and cast them in my professional career. This is followed by a student's story of how they caught actions while a team member and how they recast actions in their personal and professional life.

Hopefully, ideas within this book might inspire individuals to think of additional polarities that fit their own unique situations. If so, I'd like to hear about them from readers. I'd also appreciate knowing if the 12 pairs of actions discussed in this book help people see more clearly and feel more passionately the happenings in their lives.* My hope is that readers will come to realize that mutually interdependent people can take positive actions that enhance their own and other's development.

Even though our program experiences were in an academic setting, I believe that ideas contained here have broader relevance to the larger public. Single women and men, couples, parents, grandparents who are in the roles of teachers, counselors, coaches, homemakers, consultants, clergy, directors, managers, physicians, secretaries, attorneys, and volunteers, all of whom may mentor people every day, can learn something from these occurrences. Most of all, I want this book to instill in others the thought that through mentoring others you too can be giving much and gaining more.

—Emily M. Wadsworth
Retired Administrator
Engineering Mentoring Programs
Purdue University

---

* Send suggestions regarding additional polarities and other reactions to Dr. Emily Wadsworth, c/o Purdue University Press, 1207 South Campus Courts—E. West Lafayette, IN 47907-1207, or email to pupress@purdue.edu

One

Welcoming/Excluding

MEANINGS

Welcoming is being genuinely receptive to other people. It means cordially greeting and receiving others. When one is welcoming, one is curious about others, one is inviting to others, one includes others. A person who is welcoming is receptive to change, to becoming increasingly aware of self and others, and open to learning from others. Established residents can be welcoming to new families who move into their neighborhoods.

Excluding is the opposite of welcoming and it occurs when people deliberately shut out other people and avoid contacts. When one is excluding, one refuses to consider others, one is uninviting to others, one banishes others. A person who excludes can feel isolated, fearful of change, or dreading the thought of existing any differently. Organizations and social groups that exclude people still exist in societies today.

CATCHING AND CASTING ACTIONS

Emy's Story

Personally, I learned the art of welcoming from my parents. My father, a Professor of Electrical Engineering, acted as advisor for the internationally composed Cosmopolitan Club at Cornell University and he modeled being receptive to people from all corners of the world. My mother was gracious when greeting students who belonged to this club as they came to our home. The result was their children never expected people to look, talk, eat, or believe the same. I learned that a great richness in my parent's life came from their receptiveness to different human beings. Throughout my adult life it has been my choice to follow the lead of my parents. I have sought out and embraced people from other cultures, visited them in their countries, and opened our homes to them for over forty years. When I have been excluded in personal situations, I have come to understand that people who are unable to welcome others are usually frightened of differences, they want to protect where they are, what they have, and how they exist. This way of thinking and being is usually an attempt to maintain a tolerable status quo, yet it can also lead to a decline in the number and quality of one's human relationships. My movement in life has always been an attempt to increase and grow through human relationships.

Professionally, I have observed many people as they interacted in homes, at schools, in places of worship, and at community meetings. I always tried to react with respect and appreciation when others welcomed me, which made me feel good, relaxed, and open. I was determined to create a like situation for other people if I ever was in a position of leadership. When the WIEP opportunity came, my entire staff realized that if we were truly welcoming to participants, then they in turn might be welcoming to each other. We made certain that our programs were inclusive: participants, team members, and speakers needed to represent the diversity of backgrounds present at our institution. Purdue University's Graduate Mentoring Program, in particular, welcomed participants from every field of engineering and included women from countries throughout the world. This was a bonus for all since *the program offered everyone involved the chance to become familiar with people from many cultures, which could assist individuals later on as professionals in a global workforce.*

CATCHING AND RECASTING ACTIONS

Siddika's Story

Did you ever feel that you could be just yourself within a special group of friends and that you were welcomed and accepted just for being you? Did you ever long to meet this special group of friends with whom you could share your joys, frustrations, ideas, to hear how they are doing, to tell how you are doing, and to be recharged to conquer it all? Did you ever feel so happy, good, and safe with this group that you missed seeing them? That is exactly how I felt while participating in the Graduate Mentoring Program at Purdue University—just being myself at a place far away from my hometown.

My introduction to the Graduate M&M Program was as a participant at their kick-off meeting in my first semester as a graduate student at Purdue University the fall of 1994. I was both excited and a bit nervous to see what would happen at the first meeting. I was hoping that I would be able to meet some female graduate students, learn from them, and fit into a group. Little did I know that I was going to feel very comfortable with this group and that every month I would be looking forward to attending another meeting to feel "safe at home" with my new friends.

The monthly Graduate M&M meetings were very well organized. The first meeting was no exception and left me with vivid fond
memories. The Graduate M&M staff members and Dr. Emily Wadsworth (Emy) were genuinely welcoming of all participants. In turn,
their warm greetings were embraced and mirrored by program participants. I especially appreciated this receptivity because the program included women from different nationalities and backgrounds.
Having grown up in another country, Turkey, I always appreciated
and noted when anyone tried to include me and genuinely showed an
interest in my culture, my background, me. This was what I was used
to seeing at my parents' house. They had taught my brother, sister,
and me the importance of truly welcoming, greeting, learning from,
and sharing with our local and international guests. So, I sympa-
thized with those who may have felt awkward in a new setting. Since
I have been there several times myself, while away on my own from
my family, I know the agony of trying to figure out if I really belonged.
The environment at the M&M meetings facilitated participants coming to know each other. Each person was paired with another within
groups and each received a heartfelt welcome and introduction to the
program and its participants. It just felt good and rewarding to be
present. At the first meeting I met great people. To this day I cherish
the friendships born from these cordial beginnings.

My experience as a program participant and later as a staff
member for the Graduate Mentoring Program allowed me to grow
personally and academically. I must admit, at times graduate school
was a roller coaster ride. I would question. . . Do I really want to
pursue an advanced degree? Is becoming a graduate civil engineer
what I really want to achieve in life? I was able to answer these questions and many more with the guidance of Emy, graduate friends,
and family. One important conclusion I was able to derive at Purdue
at the culmination of my tenure as a staff member was that I wanted

to touch people's lives. One way to accomplish this goal was by mentoring others. To be a good mentor, I learned to be welcoming, open, respectful, trustworthy, and appreciative of others in addition to allowing myself to be mentored for my continued growth.

When I needed to talk to someone, M&M staff members and Dr. Wadsworth greeted me with an unconditional welcome. I was able to share my frustrations and confusions along with joys. I received and learned the power of affirmation. Inwardly, I learned to welcome the new dreams I wanted to pursue and goals I wanted to achieve in my life. With the help of Emy, one particularly close staff member, friends, my boyfriend (who later became my husband), and my family, I was able to refocus my thinking and channel my energy in a positive way to persevere in my study and go after my dreams.

The Graduate M&M Program enabled me to enlist the support of special people who touched my life. My family is and has always been very supportive of me. My parents and siblings have encouraged, affirmed, and believed in me. They have been there for me all the time. However, when one is far away from home, one does not have the comfort of readily seeking out family's help. Hence, the welcome I received at the mentoring program meant a great deal. It translated into encouragement and joy to carry on at school. The welcome, spreading like an epidemic, naturally begot an incessant support group for all program participants. Like many other female engineering students within the program, I persevered through my graduate studies. The goal of the Graduate M&M program was to increase the number of graduate degrees for female engineering students. The unconditional welcome encouraged participants to attend meetings, persist in their studies, and finally obtain their advanced degrees. The welcome was truly beneficial for all participants, assisting them in achieving their own desires while helping to realize the overall program goal.

Since graduating from Purdue University, I have been working in a multinational company that has a diverse mosaic of employees and clients. Being welcoming of all is a critical characteristic to heed and practice for every employee in our company. This skill, along with others I had sharpened as a Graduate M&M participant and M&M staff member at Purdue University, positioned me to be recognized in my company as an able leader and engineer. Hence I was invited to serve on the Diversity Advisory Council and several other initiatives at work. These visible leadership positions allowed me to share my experiences with others. In these numerous leadership roles, I was invited to speak about being an engineer to countless numbers of middle and high school students, Girl Scouts, parents and co-workers. At these speaking engagements, I tried to touch lives by sharing what I learned from my mentors and personal insights. I did my best to welcome all individuals as persons of worth. First, I laid the foundation for a mutual learning experience for everyone. I conveyed knowledge and in a turn-taking process I myself gained knowledge from others. At meetings, I made great professional and personal friends. I gained new mentors and met new mentees. To this day, I keep in touch with all of these friends. I have found out that nurturing human relationships is an enriching journey both professionally and personally. There is so much we can learn from each other through sharing.

Outside of work I have had a chance to serve as an officer in numerous volunteer engineering and cultural organizations. I served as President of the Society of Women Engineers (SWE) Houston Area Section. Both WIEP and SWE have been extremely welcoming of my potential and me. These groups are receptive to what I can offer and share. They have been instrumental in my development as a better human being, an engineer and a leader. Both of these organizations essentially serve the same purpose in academia and professional life: To stimulate women and students to achieve full potential in school and careers as engineers and leaders, expand the image of the engineering profession as a positive force, and demonstrate the value of diversity.

Through several of the SWE outreach programs I have mentored middle and high school students. Some of these students had not been given a chance to prove themselves in their environments due to family and financial hardships. Through mentoring and diligent work, it is amazing how one can shape, open, and expand new horizons for young minds. One student who was mentored by my SWE fellows and me impressed us at a scholarship reception. She delivered a speech welcoming new students and encouraging them to embrace new ideas and to be embraced by people around them. She concluded that she had soared to new heights by doing this herself.

Although I try my best to be inclusive in a team environment, I did encounter exclusion in the workplace. At an early stage of my professional career, I had to gather my courage and resolve an undesirable situation. It was disturbing because I had to step out of my comfort zone. I explained the situation to my co-worker with whom I was having difficulty. Initiating open, honest communication and establishing a platform for mutual trust and respect enabled our concerns to be addressed effectively. The issue was resolved immediately. In this instance, I learned that being open does not mean making yourself vulnerable. Being open means being more confident and peaceful with yourself.

In my leadership roles in community organizations outside of my work, I have had the pleasure of mentoring young professional women. I always appreciated it (and still do) when I was greeted with open arms in meetings and given a chance to participate. I try to practice the same philosophy when I interact with people around me. I have seen several competent leaders shine and soar in volunteer organizations as a result of this philosophy. I especially feel rewarded when I see that a warm welcome that was passed on to me is passed on to others by my mentee.

Welcoming versus excluding can make a big impact on one's life. By greeting and including others, you make yourself and your surroundings comfortable, thereby creating an environment for mutual recall and learning. The possibilities of new beginnings, horizons, and relationships are boundless when experiences are shared. There is no end to learning and there is so much we can glean from each other! So surrender yourself and let your soul be arrested by a warm welcome. Reach out to people, inspirations, and ideas! Make yourself and others feel safe at home with each welcome you receive and give! Remember to celebrate the power and boundless possibilities of each welcome shared!

SIDDIKA DEMIR received her BS degree in Civil Engineering in 1993 from the University of Houston and her MS degree in Civil Engineering from Purdue University in 1996. She is employed as a civil engineer, in the position of Six Sigma Black Belt, for Bechtel Corporation. She is married to Emre Velipasaoglu, who also graduated from Purdue with MS and PhD degrees in Electrical Engineering and is now working for Enkata Technologies.

Two

Communicating/Bickering

MEANINGS

Communicating means listening carefully, reflecting clearly, then integrating feedback. It involves taking turns in conversations; you talk and I will listen, then I talk and you listen. Both people need to maintain eye contact, be attentive to the other, and act as a mirror for the other. Restating what was said by the other person and vice versa helps to check out whether each has heard the other accurately. Communication is helped if one is comfortable with oneself and encourages the other person to also feel the same way.

Bickering means quarreling and squabbling with others. This usually occurs when people are agitated about, disrespectful of, and demeaning to one another. They ignore and/or refuse to listen to what each other is saying. Such people rarely ask questions for clarification and apparently do not want a clearer understanding of comments made. They seem to enjoy bickering more than searching for a solution.

CATCHING AND CASTING ACTIONS

Emy's Story

I never grasped how to communicate effectively until I was in my graduate studies. I took courses in human development and discovered that listening and reflecting were important aspects of communicating. Each time I spoke with people, I tried to spend equal amounts of time on both aspects and expected them to do the same. I practiced these newfound techniques with my husband and four children with varying results. Some were draws where we each timidly tried for a few minutes to inform one another. A few were losses where we ended up bickering and dumping on each other. Some were wins where we truly heard the other. It has taken years for me to become skilled at communicating.

Good communication is necessary for effective individual or group performance. I knew our team members could improve their communication by using reality checks. This means that people needed to check with others to find out *if* what they themselves thought happened in a given situation was like what others perceived in the same situation. *Giving and receiving feedback became vital to our programs.* I encouraged team members for the two Undergraduate Mentoring Programs to develop and send out a brief monthly email message titled the M&M Minute to all program participants. The message incorporated announcements, strategies, and lots of encouragement along with requests for replies, suggestions, and student concerns. At first there were disputes about what to include in the messages and griping about having to take the time to compose them. Although the attempt was slow in taking off, gradually team members reached out more and more and participants responded. This feedback loop led to refinements in the programs such as involving participants in generating questions for upcoming speakers.

CATCHING AND RECASTING ACTIONS

Betsy's Story

"Stop bickering girls," an instruction from my mother to my younger sister and me as the two of us "discussed" such important childhood concerns such as who gets to go first in a game of Candy Land. This was one of my first lessons in effective communication. From an early age, I learned that bickering was counterproductive and never resolved anything, and that effective communication came from both talking and listening. Over the years, I developed the ability to communicate with others, but little did I know that when I joined the Mentoring Program Staff Team, my communication skills were about to be taken to a higher level.

Communication is critical to the development and nurturing of mentoring relationships, as well as to planning and implementing an effective mentoring program. Staff members, under the guidance of Dr. Emily Wadsworth, were given explicit instructions and expectations regarding both oral and written communication. For example, Emy provided each team member with a binder containing staff and program materials such as a description of duties and a schedule of events. Additionally, effective communication was cast indirectly by modeling the action. An experienced team member would facilitate the first staff meeting of the fall semester in order to demonstrate communication for newer staff members. The role of facilitator was then rotated among all staff members throughout the school year at staff meetings and monthly gatherings.

Other examples of communication used with staff members included meeting agendas, follow-up memos, and copies of the minutes from weekly meetings. In conjunction with the mentoring program, monthly surveys were used to obtain participant feedback, which was used to continually improve the program. A compilation of monthly survey results and program retention rates were included in year-end reports sent to deans and foundation officers, which proved to be critical in receiving continued funding for the program. To ensure regular communication with program participants, each staff member served as a contact person to a designated group of participants. Staff members regularly emailed and called program participants to advise them of upcoming events and to chat. Through my experience as a staff member, I learned that effective communication means clearly stating my ideas and opinions, listening carefully, valuing others' opinions and ideas, and asking for clarification when necessary.

The communication skills I gained while serving on the M&M Program Staff Team have benefited me in personal relationships with friends and family. Over the years, I discovered that the root of most problems in relationships was miscommunication, so I strive to listen to and speak honestly with friends and family. Some pertinent examples of effective communication in personal relationships are the interactions between my husband and me. We strive to exchange thoughts and feelings clearly to prevent misunderstandings from occurring. However, when misunderstandings occur, we never shout or raise our voices at each other, rather we seriously discuss the issue using "I" statements as opposed to "you" statements. We take turns listening and talking, aiming to understand and respect the other's viewpoint. Effective daily communication and resolution of conflicts has resulted in the tremendous joy of sharing life with each other.

The mentoring program's successes were due in part to effective communication among staff members when executing a well-organized program as previously described, and through regular exchanges between staff and program participants. Phone calls and emails to program participants expressed the importance of the individual to the staff member and program. Additionally, implementation of survey suggestions and involvement of participants in monthly meetings, such as recognition of special events and accomplishments, provided participants with a sense of "ownership" in the program. These feelings of importance to and ownership in the program led to increased attendance at monthly meetings that benefited all present with additional mentoring experiences. Results of the M&M Programs, disseminated to university administrators through year-end reports, led to their institutionalization in 1998. More than a thousand students have benefited from all three mentoring programs over time.

My professional experience with communication is comprised of the time I spent pursuing my Ph.D. in engineering. This particular action has played a critical role in my achievements as I exchanged ideas, thoughts, and opinions with professors, industry professionals, fellow graduate students, and undergraduate students during numerous conversations and emails. One of the most enlightening communication experiences in graduate school was the exchange of information with international students and professors. During conversations with these people, I learned a great deal about life around the world and fine-tuned my own language skills while conversing with those for whom English was a second language.

Effective communication with professors and industry professionals has been critical to my success in coursework, development of my research project, and presentation of my research results. I have further developed my written and oral communication skills when writing publications and giving conference presentations. One of the most challenging presentations I gave was at an international conference in Helsinki, Finland. My audience consisted of experts in my field from Europe, Australia, and North America. To give a quality presentation, I added a little humor; avoided confusing phrases and jargon; made simple, clear slides; and carefully articulated my words. The use of these techniques led to a well-received presentation.

As my major professor's research group grew in size, group meetings became disorganized and time was wasted jumping from one topic to another and back to the first. I suggested that one person facilitate each meeting on a rotating basis and that the facilitator prepare a one-page summary reporting each researcher's progress to improve meeting efficiency and productivity. As a result of these changes, meetings were more informative and concise.

During my graduate studies, I have had the opportunity to mentor undergraduate students conducting research in the laboratory of my major professor. My role as a mentor included articulating the goals of the research project, overseeing progress, serving as a consultant, and grading reports and presentations. Following the model I experienced as a M&M Staff Member, I set forth expectations in writing and discussed these with students, met regularly with each student to monitor her/his progress, and required regular progress reports. I also made the time to get to know each student on a more personal level, inquiring about what were his/her outside interests, how did she/he get interested in food engineering research, what were his/her plans after graduation, etc. Knowing a little more about each student made my job as a mentor more interesting and helped me to understand and appreciate the work of each person. Through these mentoring experiences, I learned that communication on both the professional and personal levels aids in the development of a meaningful mentoring relationship.

From early comments made by my mother, direct and indirect actions taken while part of the M&M Program Staff, and personal mistakes and professional successes, I have learned that communication plays a critical role in happiness. My life has been enriched through mentoring relationships, and communication has been critical to the success of these relationships. As I look to the future, I eagerly await new mentoring possibilities and opportunities to continue to improve my communication skills.

BETSY WILLIS received both her BS and PhD degrees, in the area of Food Process Engineering, from Purdue University, the first in December 1996 and the second in August 2001. She is presently a Fellow of the Institute for Engineering Education at Southern Methodist University. Betsy is married to David Willis, who has his MS and PhD degrees in Mechanical Engineering from Purdue University and is now an Assistant Professor of Mechanical Engineering at Southern Methodist University.

Three

Trusting/Doubting

MEANINGS

Trusting is having confidence in the reliability of another person. It also relates to accepting both the positive and negative attributes of a person, for certain characteristics may be unchangeable. It is imperative that we trust ourselves first then pass it on to others. Trusting implies that we believe in the honesty, integrity, responsibility, loyalty, and dependability of another human being. We need to model these characteristics ourselves before we can expect them from others. If we feel a sense of loyalty to people, we will be there for each other during times of disappointment and loss as well as during times of delight and gain.

Doubting is being unsure about the reliability of another person. If we doubt another human being, we might question his or her honesty, be reluctant to swap intimacies, and be uncertain about whether he or she can be held accountable.

CATCHING AND CASTING ACTIONS

Emy's Story

Early on in my personal life I was taught to be trustworthy, to be responsible for myself and my siblings, to be there for each other. All during childhood and adulthood I have lived with the certainty that my sisters and brother would support me during sorrowful and joyful periods. They have been anchors for me, providing the stability I needed whenever it was needed. I have been able to count on them, and they on me. We have believed in each other and appreciated each other's uniqueness. Individually and collectively we have struggled with our development. We are independent as well as interdependent. *We grew up accepting the idea that when trusting one another, no one had a vested interest in changing the other.* We support each other's freedom to become what we were meant to be.

My university positions over two decades led me to develop small support groups and use student teams to assist me with teaching, research, and administrative responsibilities. During weekly gatherings there would be team-building exercises to help us transition into meetings, forget outside distractions, and focus on programs. An instance related to trusting and doubting would be having members complete statements defining what these words meant to them. After writing down definitions, we would share responses, discuss various aspects of trusting and doubting, and suggest actions we could take to create an environment of reliability within our teams. Collectively the Mentoring Program Staff Teams passed this learning on to participants by initiating sharing times. These moments involved students' communicating about happenings such as passing exams, enjoying semester breaks, or obtaining internships. Group cohesion was visibly affected when team members occasionally missed weekly sessions and program participants decided not to be present at monthly gatherings. Staff and participants started letting absent people know through various contacts that they missed them when they weren't there. The result was higher weekly attendance rates, increased monthly participation, less doubting and more trusting among all concerned.

CATCHING AND RECASTING ACTIONS

Marlee's Story

Trust was honestly something that I took for granted before college. I was fortunate enough never to have had reason to doubt my parents or their love for me. I was comfortable with the trust they placed in me to be a positive role model for my two younger sisters. I had plenty of great friends, was active in many extracurricular activities, and academics had never been difficult for me. I had never been really let down. I was a Good Kid with a Bright Future. After graduation, I packed away my valedictorian stole and homecoming queen crown without a doubt in my mind that the pursuit of an engineering degree at Purdue University would mean more of the same.

How things change when a girl has to walk the tightrope without a safety net! I believe that it is difficult to fully know an action without appreciating its counteraction, so perhaps I was lucky to experience a generous dose of doubt during my sophomore year at Purdue. It started with a seemingly minor event. I was invited to interview for a summer internship, but the interview was scheduled at the same time as my weekly staff meeting for the M&M Mentoring Program. I figured that this would be an excused absence, but I neglected to explain why I missed the meeting until after the fact. In her always-gentle way, Dr. Wadsworth (Emy) explained that she understood if I needed to miss a meeting from time to time, but that it was crucial to let the team know of the circumstances and of the progress made on my assignments beforehand. People were counting on me to help plan this program. This quiet, kind-hearted reproach hit me hard. Had I let someone down? Was I really capable of giving my team reason to doubt my reliability, loyalty, or dependability?

While this was a pretty minor incident, it was very significant in teaching me something about trust and about working on a team. I realized that these people, and all the others with whom I would work in the future, were not obligated to trust me on my own good name.

There were harder knocks that year to further deepen my self-doubt: a three-year relationship with my first serious boyfriend ended and my perfect grade-point average took a significant nosedive with chemical engineering classes.

Through these setbacks, another lesson was learned: sharing doubts dispelled them. I had a support group made up of my family and friends. One of the most important members of that support group was Emy. She constantly reinforced the fact that I could make it in engineering and that I was a multidimensional, unique person with something to give to the world.

Make it through I did, but I don't think many mortals can make it through an engineering program alone. Group design and laboratory projects are a major part of the curriculum, and there is too much work involved in them for one person to do it all. The way forward is for each person to do his or her own section with the best possible effort. I found that my group work was most successful and enjoyable when I could trust my ability to contribute to the project and when I could trust my teammates to do the same. This principle was perfected in our mentoring program staff, and I think that's why we were able to implement such a fun and valuable program. I believe that our trust in one another and in ourselves was evident to the participants. There were virtually no unexcused absences from the program once we established a specific staff member as a contact person for each participant. The women in the group knew they were depended upon; they knew that the staff and their mentor/ mentee trusted them to be present for and to contribute to the meetings, and they did not want their reliability to be doubted.

I believe this lesson in trust and reliability directly related to persistence in the pursuit of an engineering degree for these women. We could trust each other to give support when we needed it; when we were in the role of the support giver, it made us see that another could be trusted. We were making a difference in others' lives, and our self-trust grew. I had the opportunity to witness M&M participants growing in trust of themselves and one another when I returned as a speaker after graduation. I went back three different years to give presentations titled "Working In a Global Environment," "Life After College," and "A Mentoring Workshop." I saw mentor/mentee pairs with obvious trust in one another, particularly when I was at Purdue later in the year and their relationships had had time to grow. I tried to stress the importance of trusting in each of my program presentations. For example, I related how self-trust helped me through the challenges of an international work assignment and how trust of others is vital in mentoring relationships.

From what I have seen, trust only becomes more important in the professional world. Teams tend to be cross functional in nature; they differ from college groups in that in many cases, a person can't even double-check a co-worker's contribution to a project even if this is what he or she wants.

I believe that the importance of trust is recognized in many corporate environments; my company frequently sponsors team-building events off-site. Sometimes there are non-work-related physical and/or mental challenges that force people to trust one another and enable them to work together more effectively when they return to the office.

Fast-paced timelines are a way of life, and competitors don't frequently give extensions. Team members who doubt one another and are unable to trust one another's commitment, expertise, or motives not only have trouble successfully completing a project, but they have a miserable time in the process.

Of course, the basis for trusting members of a team is in trusting oneself. Mentors and support groups can certainly reinforce this trust. To form truly synergistic, rewarding relationships—both professional and personal—an individual must be able to feel the strength of the talent, will, and character deep within herself. Doubt should be appreciated because it can force us to look at ourselves and improve areas in which we are not confident. While it's easy to trust when you've never doubted, it's most important to trust once you have.

MARLEE JANSEN graduated from Purdue University in 1997 with a BS degree in Chemical Engineering. She then worked for Kimberly-Clark Corporation as an international product developer. In August 2001, she began law school at the University of Minnesota.

Four

Accepting/Rejecting

MEANINGS

Accepting involves approving of people for what they are and where they are. When people are accepting, they realize they will encounter differences of opinion, conflicts of interests, and frictions of many kinds between people. Through these encounters they can begin to learn how to tolerate one another's weaknesses and appreciate one another's strengths. This is a long-term process that generally involves small steps forward and lots of backsliding.

Rejecting involves treating people as worthless and useless. When people are rejecting, they have a hard time acknowledging that everyone should have an equal opportunity to express opinions and concerns. Such people will negate comments by others and might consider them to be personal slights or insults. Students of any age who are blatantly rejecting of their peers can be insecure and unable to tolerate their own weaknesses and life's limits.

CATCHING AND CASTING ACTIONS

Emy's Story

Upon graduating from Cornell University, I moved with my husband to a small village. The rural people there were a sharp contrast to the urban people in the city where I was raised. This led to my having difficulty transitioning to the new location and to people living there. At first I only related to a few friends with whom there was a common background, then I ventured forth and joined some groups. After several months of being involved in community affairs, the realization dawned on me that many of the villagers were more differentiated than I, meaning their movement toward maturity was far beyond my own. Despite my initial rebuffs and immature manners, villagers came to accept me and I in turn came to appreciate their skills and personalities. I have used this humbling experience to urge our children to open themselves up to other human beings, to learn from them in whatever they may be doing and wherever they exist.

I first encountered the concept of depersonalization in graduate school and later during my years as an educator and counselor. When professors critiqued my work, feelings of defensiveness and devastation surfaced inside of me. Over time, I came to view their analyses as a tremendous way to obtain feedback that could improve my professional endeavors. When I finally understood what they were doing and why, it involved a traumatic and gratifying turn in my thinking that led to depersonalizing: separating my sense of self from other people's remarks. Meeting with team members and participants over the course of a decade, the understanding came that many were, as I had been, negatively affected by any form of constructive critique. They would feel hurt, slighted, rejected. We started discussing the idea of depersonalization both individually and during team meetings. I encouraged them to perceive of professional reviews as opportunities for growth and wanted them to realize that *people are entitled to their opinions and we are challenged to grasp those opinions instead of rejecting them.* I explained that several reasons for letting one's work be critiqued might be to enlarge one's scope of thinking and make connections between ideas that might never have been considered. Throughout one's entire career a valuable asset can be having trusted peers review one's work.

CATCHING AND RECASTING ACTIONS

Lina's Story

I really think that one of the major influences on our self-esteem is whether we feel accepted or rejected by others. I can't imagine anyone being excluded from the positive impact of acceptance or the negative feeling of rejection. We may have experienced this as young children in gym class waiting for the team captain to call our name and pick us for his kickball team, hoping we wouldn't be the last kid to be picked. Maybe in high school we had a teacher who showed acceptance by patting us on the back with a "job well done" or maybe we experienced rejection by not making the cuts for the basketball team. In college, we may have enjoyed acceptance by a group of friends in a club or organization or suffered rejection by a prospective boyfriend or girlfriend. We even experience the two actions of accepting and rejecting in the workplace. We encounter higher job satisfaction when our bosses and co-workers show acceptance of us and our work through words of affirmation and praise (and especially promotions!). At other times, we may feel rejected in the workplace when we are given critical feedback on our performance or when a raise we were expecting to receive isn't given to us.

Personally, I have had quite a few experiences with both rejection and acceptance and have learned a great deal from each experience. As a sophomore in college, I had the privilege of being asked by Dr. Emily Wadsworth, Emy, to become part of a team that would take part in the beginning stages of a mentoring program. As new team members we shared two similarities: we were studying engineering at the same university and we were all females. However, we also had differences. We studied different fields of engineering, came to Purdue from different states, even different countries. We began creating the M&M Program through brainstorming sessions with Emy. Since we were coming from a variety of backgrounds, we discussed the importance of being open to all ideas. We were able to accomplish the task of sketching the details of the program, but there was one factor that led to team members' feeling rejected or slighted. We were a group of individuals with different personalities. There was one specific team member whose personality was very different from my own. When this individual did not joyfully support the ideas that I shared, or express enthusiasm when I joined the new team, I took her actions personally and perceived that I was being singled out. Now that I am older and have more experience, I can reflect and realize that the rejection I felt in relation to this individual probably had nothing to do with me. Instead, it might have come about as a result of variations in our personalities. The other team member was more reserved and focused on self whereas I was more high-spirited and concerned with group harmony. Because I did not fully comprehend what was happening at the time, I let myself be intimidated by her and was unable to be accepting of her.

Staff members continued to grow and mature over the course of several semesters. I was fortunate to receive acceptance by teammates, not only as a peer who contributed to the monthly meetings, but also as an individual who had abilities and friendship to offer outside of the meeting environment. I specifically remember one occasion when Emy asked me to sing a song at the holiday social gathering she hosted each year. I had recently auditioned for one of the much-desired solos that were part of the Purdue Musical Organizations Christmas Show. Just like the year before, someone else in the organization was selected to perform this particular solo. I was disappointed and felt that my singing talent was being rejected. Once again, I failed to understand that it wasn't me or my skill that was being questioned; instead, someone else's voice provided the needed sound for a specific solo part. When I finished singing "Chestnuts Roasting" for my peers at the holiday social, I received applause that assured me that all present accepted and appreciated my musical talent. That was good enough for me.

There were many instances when the mentoring program staff members sought feedback from participants regarding specific portions of monthly gatherings. It was through my reviewing of these evaluations that Emy introduced me to the idea of depersonalization. I had no idea at the time how learning this skill would prove to be valuable to me during my college years and in other relationships after graduation. Depersonalization allowed me the chance to remove myself from critical feedback regarding the mentoring program, not take student comments personally, and view negative remarks as indications that program changes might be needed.

As part of the staff of the M&M program and also as a female engineering student myself, I knew how important it was to create an environment of acceptance for participants in the program. The M&M monthly meetings were events where a female engineering student could find support and encouragement through speakers, staff members, and other participants. Our hope was that this support would help those involved persist in college and graduate with BS degrees. We knew that if there was acceptance of each participant at program meetings, then an individual could be inspired to return to future meetings and gain more encouragement. I personally came to realize that it was necessary for me to put aside my own daily concerns like upcoming tests and responsibilities I had with other campus organizations and focus on showing acceptance towards participants at these meetings. If I didn't do this, my personal distractions could come across to others as a form of rejection, possibly deterring students from further participation.

I had the opportunity to "fine tune" my depersonalization skills upon graduation as I accepted and began a position as a manufacturing supervisor for Intel Corporation. I entered this position and work environment a bit of a "softy." Remember that I liked harmonious atmospheres where there was concern for other people's feelings. Overall, the company stressed a positive message of acceptance for employees, which I experienced from day one with my peer supervisors. It was through this team of approximately seven supervisors that I saw for the first time how powerful teamwork could be in the workplace. Thinking back, I recognize that our teamwork was effective because we sustained a positive work setting and were accepting of each other as individuals. We had been trained to foster such an environment and to refrain from tapping into rejection and getting personal.

A very important tool we learned to use was the concept of constructive confrontation. Confronting differences in a constructive way allowed us to exercise accountability and address varying ideas, opinions, and behaviors without being discrediting. Using constructive confrontation and depersonalization helped me to perform more successfully in my work as a manufacturing supervisor. My anxiety was diminished in certain situations, as when I needed to deliver a negative message (such as a less than acceptable performance evaluation) to a peer or a subordinate. By the time I left my supervisory position and company to enter the full-time profession of motherhood, I had transitioned from a "softy" who avoided conflict so my feelings wouldn't get hurt to someone who used feedback (solicited or unsolicited) to improve who I was as a person.

Even though my experiences at Intel were centered mostly on acceptance, I observed the action of rejection through my relationship with a specific individual in upper management. The employee I am referring to was very accepting of peers and subordinates if their personalities, interests, and viewpoints were similar to his own. On the other hand he was very rejecting of people at work if their personalities, interests, and viewpoints were different from his own. Due to his "selective acceptance" and because of his high position in the management hierarchy, our team members experienced frustration and sometimes division in the workplace. Although at times this particular manager had a negative impact on our team, I did learn from him how critical it is to make the necessary effort to accept others who are different from us.

Accepting has become very important to me as I mature in my roles as an individual, a wife, mother, and friend. I recently learned the term "Grace Space" which, to me, means graciously giving someone else "space" or "permission" to be different than me and accepting them in spite of these differences. I would even go one step further and state that this acceptance occurs only when you truly assess and understand who you are as an individual. Stop and ask yourself, "What are my interests, behaviors, preferences, and goals? What are my strengths and weaknesses?" After understanding more of what you are doing and where you are going, you will be better equipped to not only accept another person who is very unlike yourself, but you will hopefully be more open to learn from each other. We can apply these actions to various aspects of our lives. Personally, acceptance can lead to stronger marriages, better understanding of children's behaviors, and growth in friendships. Professionally, acceptance can build stronger and more balanced teams, lead to increased production from employees, and establish rich mentor-mentee relationships.

I would summarize all my experiences and resultant learning about acceptance and rejection by stating that everybody is different and there really isn't any way we can fully understand another human being. If we stop trying to change others to be like us, we can not only accept them, but also appreciate them, differences and all.

LINA MARTIN received her BS in Industrial Engineering from Purdue University in 1994. She and her husband, Joel, a mechanical engineer and fellow Purdue graduate, then accepted positions with Intel Corporation. Presently, Lina is a full-time mother caring for their two young daughters and she is acting as a mentor in her community.

Five

Affirming/Ridiculing

MEANINGS

Affirming is praising people for attributes, which can further their development. By affirming another person, we declare that the other has strengths and that we appreciate these strengths. Affirmation will generally heighten the self-esteem and increase the confidence of individuals.

Ridiculing is mocking people, which can inhibit their development. If we mock another person, we browbeat, jeer, and bully to show our disapproval. We focus on weaknesses instead of strengths.

CATCHING AND CASTING ACTIONS

Emy's Story

One of the strongest parental messages I ever received in childhood was *You can do it!* I believed this as I achieved in school and musical activities during elementary, junior, and senior high schools. I continued to be confident of my abilities in college. Then, after I married, my mate further reinforced and assured me of my capabilities to the point where he urged me to return for advanced degrees. His willingness to prepare meals, his confirmation of my progress, and his affirmation of my uniqueness provided needed physical, mental, and emotional sustenance during trying times. He, more than anyone else, showed me that *when people strengthen others they inwardly strengthen themselves.* My attainment of degrees and subsequent university positions were exterior outcomes.

Numerous times throughout my professional career, I found myself repeating to discouraged and disillusioned women the phrase *You can do it!*

When someone believed in them and counterbalanced the disapproval they were experiencing as students, then they also came to believe in themselves and others. I learned over eight years of the mentoring programs that if we included participants in assisting us at monthly meetings, then they might feel a sense of program ownership and this in turn could lead to greater program commitment. This was a key play! We began by requesting undergraduate students to meet in small groups, develop a skit related to a particular topic, then offer it at monthly meetings. Likewise, we asked graduate students to give presentations on their research topics and answer questions from participants. Sometimes the events bombed and students felt nervous and intimidated, yet they came to know that program meetings were a safe testing ground for later presentations in classrooms and at conferences. These involvements offered everyone the chance to be affirmed for her contribution to the program. We acknowledged that people at times felt awkward when praised or complimented. At weekly team meetings we had instances when we practiced hearing, accepting, and appreciating affirmation from others. At times it was difficult, yet we knew that when endorsing and actively supporting one another, we were having the opportunity to model the art of mentoring and practice the art of affirming, which could enrich our professional and personal lives.

CATCHING AND RECASTING ACTIONS

Leah's Story

I was four years old standing on the edge of the diving board crying. I could feel the other kids staring at me, the "crybaby" of the class. I focused down at the water and dived in. Struggling with sobs between each stroke, I finally made it to the end of the pool. When I surfaced, to my amazement, I was met with hand clapping and cheering by everyone present. I did it. I did it!

Fast-forward 20 years . . . at the end of my first year of graduate school I was introduced to the Graduate Mentoring Program by Dr. Emily Wadsworth (Emy), and I immediately wanted to be a part of it, mostly because I recognized the need for such an experience in my own life. I anticipated being part of a program that would help provide guidance and direction to individuals new to the world of academia and also support more veteran students.

Affirming others was a key driver in achieving the program's goals of retaining women in engineering, and it was apparent that Emy knew the value of affirmation and understood the impact that words of encouragement can make on someone's life. Emy was a sounding board to many of the team members and we would often discuss our latest calamity with her. Most of the time difficulties were fueled by uncertainty in our own capabilities, and Emy would provide the affirmation that we needed with an outspoken "You can do it!" I would always leave conversations with Emy feeling empowered and capable of taking on the world.

Unfortunately "You can do it!" were not words spoken by my advisor or other professors, and upon returning to my daily environment, I would revert to my own lack of self-confidence. Luckily conversations and interactions with friends and family restored the balance in my mind concerning my own abilities. My parents were very supportive of my endeavors from my high school years into my academic career, where I found that I needed affirmation from them more and more. I remember feeling very low after not performing very well on one of my first engineering exams and talking with my parents over the phone about it almost in tears. After calming me down, my parents affirmed my abilities. Collectively we devised a plan for me to meet with the professor during office hours and to work with a study group. With their support and guidance and a lot of hard work on my part, I received an A in the course. Although I relied on my parents' affirmation for most of my academic career, little by little, with each accomplishment, my self-esteem increased and I was more able to rely on myself for support.

In relation to the Graduate Mentoring Program Emy affirmed our abilities not only through words, but also through her actions. She empowered team members by making them responsible for the plans and execution of monthly events. As team members we would rotate facilitating responsibilities for weekly meetings and tasks for the monthly gatherings, which ensured everyone had an opportunity to utilize and develop different skills and interact with program participants. This demonstrated her faith in us to make the program a success and also resulted in strengthening the staff team. Emy also supported us by affirming attributes that she believed were unique to us as individuals. She would highlight how these attributes made us valuable as a person and team member. I remember Emy telling me once that she thought I had a gift as a mediator and that I provided a needed balance in our staff team, which sometimes had warring factions. I had not recognized this quality in myself, but once it was mentioned I began to take a closer look at how I interact with others. I found myself wanting to further develop these skills so that I could be more of an asset to the team.

As our graduate staff group passed through the stages of developing a team—Forming, Norming, Storming, and Performing—we unfortunately became trapped in the storming stage, in which a lot of ridiculing between team members occurred. It had been my first exposure to ridiculing since my childhood school days, and it caused me to reexamine my interactions with team members. I found that I was not comfortable associating with mocking individuals, but I was not completely comfortable associating with the individual who was being ridiculed either, probably from fear that the belittling behavior of others would be turned on me. Therefore, I found myself withdrawing from any extended interaction with the team members outside of weekly meetings. Over several months of time, Emy had individual conferences with the program staff during which she expressed her concern about negative interactions among team members and suggested ways to alleviate the ridiculing. Eventually, our team passed from the storming to the performing stage of team development.

As I became more familiar with affirming and ridiculing, it became clear that I did not want to associate or be associated with people who ridiculed others. I did not always have the strength at the time to confront individuals who were ridiculing others in my presence, but I made a choice to not participate in the conversation. I am not proud of this, but at the time, with my own insecurities, it was all I could do. It also became clear that I wanted to associate with individuals who had a positive attitude toward themselves and others, and that I wanted to strengthen my ability to be an advocate for others. For me, encouragement from my family and future husband was only a phone call away; but I had a few friends who weren't as fortunate. I therefore tried to provide the same support to them that I was able to receive. At one time a friend of mine had succumbed to ridicule that she was receiving from her advisor regarding a paper that she was writing and she was feeling very low about her abilities. By simply talking with her about her past accomplishments and her many strengths, I was able to discount the ridiculing remarks and restore her self-esteem so that she no longer dwelled on her advisor's harsh words.

The support provided through affirming others helped make the M&M Graduate Program successful. Team members received support from Emy, which fostered feelings of ownership whereby individuals strived to make the program, their program, a success. Program evaluations reaffirmed the efforts made by team members, and provided some of the most meaningful gratitude they ever received: that of our peers. The process and content of monthly meetings also affirmed program participants and team members and led to the success of the program. Each monthly meeting would feature an accomplished alumna who would address a specific topic. As these women shared their stories, participants in the program identified with the obstacles and challenges that these women overcame, and they were able to recognize their own ability to overcome similar challenges. The speakers shared specific strategies for topics such as job hunting, choosing research advisors, and balancing a family and career that provided program participants with a set of tools for dealing with these issues. One speaker emphasized the importance of talking to graduate students when choosing a research advisor to "get the professor's real story," and another speaker stressed the importance of networking with everyone when conducting a job search. Support was also given to program participants through recognition of their contributions: Research presentations were met with applause and speakers were presented with gifts of appreciation. Through the M&M Graduate Program, participants became aware that they were not alone in the challenges that they faced. They became part of a support network with other students and alumnae and were provided with a set of tools for tackling many of the obstacles that they faced. This helped to increase the participant's self-esteem and enabled them to achieve their goals.

Academia aside, there is also a strong need for affirming others in the workplace. It is especially critical for individuals who are new to an organization or assignment. In my first professional assignment I worked for a supervisor who regularly affirmed me. Knowing that he was comfortable with my abilities gave me confidence, and I was able to approach more challenging problems that might have otherwise intimidated me. For example, when faced with developing a process for a new material that involved learning a new technology, he affirmed my abilities through words and actions by giving me responsibility for completing the project and informing others of my role. Because of his words and actions I felt empowered, and therefore worked extra hard to make the project, my project, a success. From working with an affirming supervisor, I knew how his words affected my attitude and actions, and the importance of supporting and affirming others professionally. In my next assignment I worked for a supervisor who did not regularly affirm others. This assignment was a broadening position for me and required skills that I had not yet developed. Without affirmation from my supervisor, I faced my work feeling challenged, but also with uncertainty and insecurities in my abilities. As I labored on this assignment, I became concerned that I did not meet expectations and instead of strengthening my skills, I began to question my ability to perform in my new role. After several discussions with my supervisor I was able to resolve my concerns, and over time she developed the ability to affirm others, which resulted in a stronger, more self-assured project group.

Affirming others is critical to an individual's professional success and to developing strong relationships with colleagues. Today individuals are constantly faced with change whether it be working outside of their technical expertise, tackling a new project, or starting a new career. The change inevitably requires individuals to work outside of their comfort zone in which they may face their limitations, whether real or imaginary. Affirming an individual's skills enables the individual to feel re-established in his or her position and therefore, it enables that person to focus on the work at hand. For example, an experienced technician was assigned to work for me in a role completely new to him. I could sense his frustration as he tried to comprehend his new work environment and what would be expected of him. He had developed an expertise in several areas, but they were no longer necessary in his new role, which required a different set of skills. Through acknowledging his previous contributions and areas of expertise, I was able to show him that I recognized and valued his abilities. I was then able to draw a direct connection of how valuable the same abilities would be in developing the skills required in his new position. Through affirming his abilities, he became more at ease with learning the new skills and was successful in his new position.

Professionally there are several benefits that are associated with affirming others. First, you are recognized as a team player and not someone solely interested in her own welfare. Through affirming others, you show that you are comfortable with your own abilities and you recognize that a diverse set of skills is required for the successful completion of a project. Affirming others can also demonstrate that you understand what skills are valued and that you have the ability to develop others within the organization. Lastly, affirming others can highlight important skills that others possess that you might not have previously considered and that may prove to be beneficial for you to develop.

As I anxiously await the birth of my first child, I reflect on many actions that will be important in rearing a healthy child and believe that affirmation will be important from the first day of life in developing self-esteem and inter-dependence. There are many times when an individual is faced with self-doubt and is surrounded by people who ridicule, but with a network of individuals who you know support and affirm your abilities, there is no limit to what you can accomplish.

LEAH A. KENNELLY graduated with a BS degree in Chemical Engineering at Penn State University in 1993 and a MS degree in Chemical Engineering at Purdue University in 1995. Since then, she has been a research engineer in product development for Procter & Gamble Corporation. Leah is married to John Kennelly, a structural engineer, and they have recently had a son.

Six

Forgiving/Condemning

Forgiving means acknowledging imperfections in ourselves first, then accepting them in others. When someone is forgiving, they admit that they have had failures and done harm and so can more readily understand the mistakes of others. Forgiving is a dynamic with key elements such as one's will, knowledge base, ability to reconcile, and problem solving skills. These elements could involve: working with the opinions of strong people; learning how to refrain from judging others; coming up with possibilities in difficult situations; and having success with settling disputes.

Condemning means strongly disapproving of one's self, for whatever reason or sets of reasons, then passing that disapproval on to others. When someone is condemning, they find it difficult to admit their own errors and they can not be accepting of other's goofs. Such people tend to avoid failure and risk taking at all costs and at the same time they declare others guilty. They often consider themselves victims rather than effective participants in a group. Condemning happens when someone lacks the creativity to construct a positive experience and gives up!

CATCHING AND CASTING ACTIONS

Emy's Story

I have had a husband and sons as my forgiveness guides. They, along with friends and mentors, have shared their experiences with me and all have jointly helped me embrace the idea that forgiving may be the ultimate beginning for true intimacy. The only way that this would happen is if I learned to first forgive myself, then learned to forgive others. At 33 years of age, I finally started holding myself accountable for my own actions and stopped blaming other people for the things they did that had previously affected my life. Slowly an identity and acceptance of my own limitations and imperfections occurred. I realized that I possessed a strong will and could be obstinate at times. My tendency had been to quickly judge other people, take strong positions on issues, and avoid reconciling disagreements. This led to a build up of disputes that were left unsettled. The turning point came when I consciously decided that my will was out of check and in the way of reaching my own goals. I needed to bring my will under control and to put it in balance in order to attain what I really desired. My judging needed to stop, my give and take needed to increase, and my decisions on what to do in certain situations needed to undergo change. These challenges led to actions, one being the practice of not expecting too much of myself and others, and not being too hard on myself and others. Honestly, *I came to believe that my ability to love correlated with my ability to forgive.* These understandings, efforts, and beliefs helped me progress towards maturity.

I used my personal situations described above as a guide when devising WIEP retention activities for students. I wanted older, more experienced people assisting younger, less experienced people. Thus, in the Undergraduate Mentoring Programs, mentors who were junior and senior women encouraged mentees who were first and second year students. In the Graduate Mentoring Program, doctoral students sponsored master students. When we first began the programs, we matched program participants in pairs, one mentee with one mentor. I pointed out to staff members the importance of matching students according to commonalties such as mutual fields of study, special interests, and/or learning styles. However, we soon found out that matching just two people was ineffective. We made a mistake in pairing because we didn't fully consider the consequences of what might happen if a matched pair was not complementary. For example, when one of the two people was very intense while the other was very laid back, when one was usually present at meetings while the other was usually absent, when one was a responsive individual while the other was non-responsive, then these two people could end up feeling threatened, disconnected, and dismissed. We realized from studying research results that only half of all mentoring matches proved to be effective over time. Therefore, when ineffective matches occurred in our program, we assured students that it wasn't their fault and that they were still personally O.K. We suggested that they forgive one another for any disappointments and we worked at re-matching them. The second year of the mentoring programs we decided to match participants in groups of four, two mentors and two mentees. These groupings were more effective and fewer rematches occurred. Overall, we needed to keep a positive frame of mind and realize we would make mistakes. We needed to avoid condemning others, practice conflict resolution, and work at bringing harmony to our team and programs. Putting this in perspective, forgiving one another was an action that helped us to advance in many aspects of our professional development.

CATCHING AND RECASTING ACTIONS

Cecelia's Story

Striving for perfection is something that many people do, consciously or unconsciously. From a very early age, I was striving for perfection. Perfection at school, perfection at home, and perfection in athletics. This desire did not come from a parental, sibling, or other outside influence. Instead, it was a desire that came very much from my inner being. Why the desire was there, I am not quite sure. This striving for perfection has led me in many positive directions. I worked very hard in high school to accomplish all that I thought was necessary for perfection. I reached one of these goals when I became Valedictorian of my senior class. However, I was not able to accomplish all of the goals that I had set for myself and this led to feelings of condemnation of myself. My desire for perfection had helped me achieve many things, but it was also holding me back. I was never able to truly enjoy my successes until I realized the need to forgive myself for not being perfect.

My lessons in learning to forgive myself began when Dr. Emily Wadsworth (Emy) asked me to become a staff member for the Undergraduate M&M Mentoring Program. Up to my second year in college, I had continued to strive for perfection in the things I did. This need can lead to disappointment and condemning of one's self when things do not go perfectly, and we all know that things rarely go perfectly.

My first lesson in forgiving came when I was assigned the task of facilitating my first M&M program meeting. During our monthly meetings, the other three student leaders and I would rotate duties. Each month someone would be the facilitator. The duties of the facilitator entailed contacting the speaker, creating materials, and leading the monthly meeting. I remember being extremely excited about my first time as a facilitator. While all the tasks of team members were important, I felt this role was most prominent. I had been watching the other, more experienced members of the team, and was sure that I had everything organized. In addition, this was to be the biggest gathering of the school year. We were having a joint meeting with the other undergraduate mentoring program. We had special speakers for the event who were flown in by one of the corporate sponsors for the WIEP. The evening meeting took place in the elegant faculty rooms located in the Purdue Memorial Union. Staff members highly promoted this event to ensure that all of the student participants would be there. Everything was prepared ahead of time and the mentoring staff team was ready to GO. Unfortunately, the night came and the program did not go very well. One of the speakers offended students when she curtly responded to their inquiries during a question and answer session following the program presentation. Survey ratings received from program participants for this particular meeting were the lowest for the year.

I was extremely disappointed, especially in myself. I felt responsible for the evening since I had been the facilitator. Somehow, I had expected perfection from myself. I did not realize that the evening might go poorly and I might have to prevent mistakes from happening. I vividly remember going home that night and crying over the disappointment of an event that I had spent hours working on and that, in my mind, had ended up being a disaster. Several days passed before I started feeling better about the meeting. It was only through conversations with our Program Administrator, Emy, and another student team member that I finally started to see the reality of the

situation. There would have been no way for me to know how the
evening would proceed. The speakers had come highly recommended from a large corporation. Team members were confident that
the program would go well. The evening was not a reflection of me,
but was simply just "one of those things that happens."

Slowly, I started to realize that I was indeed, not perfect. I am
sure that I always knew that I was not perfect, however this experience gave me a greater understanding of myself. I started to recognize
that I did not need to be perfect either, which was probably the
greater realization. None of the participants or staff members held me
personally responsible for the way the evening had gone. They had
forgiven and forgotten about the program by the next day. I realized
it was only me that was holding myself responsible. By learning to
forgive myself, I began to see this particular event for what it really
was. The situation was a tremendous growth experience. I learned
that sometimes no matter how well one plans, something still may go
wrong; and we should not condemn ourselves for things over which
we have no control. This helped me learn to forgive other team members as well as participants in the mentoring program. Knowing how
hard I had worked for something that did not happen exactly as
planned allowed me to realize that sometimes when other people had
difficulties running meetings smoothly, it might not be from lack of
effort. This ability to forgive applied to all of the people associated
with the program and helped me to strengthen my communications
with them throughout the year.

Learning to forgive myself and, more importantly, other people
was vital to the success of the M&M Program. As staff members, we
were charged with contacting twelve of the program participants
each month. Phone calls were made just prior to a meeting as a gentle
reminder of the upcoming event. Phone calls were also made after the
monthly program if the individual had not attended and had not re-

sponded to the invitation. Phone calls after the meeting were usually the hardest to make. We knew that participants wanted to attend all meetings; however sometimes the pressure of schoolwork, exams, boyfriends, professors, friends, etc., got in the way of their other activities. It was very important not to condemn any of the participants for missing a meeting, even if the reason for their absence was simply "I forgot." The M&M Program was designed as a support group for these women. The program was a place where they could come and receive encouragement from others. It was not up to the staff or other participants to judge another person's attendance record. While we did ask for committed participation over the year, we were flexible to the needs of program participants. We realized that, like ourselves, participants might make mistakes. It was part of our job as staff members to set an example of forgiveness for all those involved with the program.

I have used my experiences as an M&M Staff Member to grow professionally. Since starting work, I have strived to become manager of a project. Over months of time, I tried to exhibit all of the needed qualities to prove to management that not only was I willing to do the job, but I was also able and prepared. Earlier this year, my opportunity to lead a project was realized. I was given a project that involved a five-person team. I was extremely excited. Then, of course, I started to get nervous. This was the first time I had managed a corporate effort. What would I do if I forgot something? How would my management react if I didn't know how to do something? Would I be able to forgive myself if I made mistakes or if the project didn't go well?

After the initial stress and shock, I reflected on what I had learned as a member of the M&M staff team. I remembered that all I could do was my best. If something did get overlooked, I would simply have to forgive myself and move on. As this story is being written, this particular project is still progressing. There are times as a manager when I have been caught off guard and there have been times when I have been completely prepared. Not only that, but there have been times when my team has been caught unprepared.

I realize that our team members work very hard and are committed to the project. I am able to forgive them for mistakes made and for not completing tasks on time. For example, a team member made a recommendation but had overlooked a key piece of data. The recommendation was therefore incorrect. The team member realized the error and approached the team with a new recommendation. We commended her for having the strength to admit the error and bring forth the correct recommendation. Lucky for me though, the forgiveness goes both ways. For example, I recently missed a meeting regarding the project. The meeting was organized by one of the team members and I felt as though I had let that person down. However, I knew that I had not intentionally missed the meeting. Likewise, the team member recognized that I was genuinely sorry for the mistake. It became a standing joke amongst the team, and I am extra careful not to miss any more meetings.

I feel fortunate to have learned the lesson of forgiveness when working on the Undergraduate Mentoring Program. I was able to stop condemning my shortcomings, forgive myself and others, celebrate my successes without guilt, and grow from my mistakes. Forgiveness has made me a more effective business leader as well as a more compassionate person.

CECELIA BERGER received her BS degree from Purdue University in 1998, majoring in the field of Chemical Engineering. After graduation, she accepted a position as a research scientist for Kimberly Clark Corporation. She spent 2001–2002 in England working in the "nappy" division of the corporation.

Seven

Reframing/Stagnating

MEANINGS

Reframing occurs when we alter our perception of a life experience and come to view it differently. It involves a change in attitude about a situation and this change might occur after some trauma or new knowledge and understanding about life. When people reframe they search for a more positive perspective than they had previously. Such people can find hope in disasters, perceive difficulties as opportunities, and comprehend that we may be most receptive to change when we are at our wit's end! Nurses have observed patients reframing their physical conditions, viewing them as new challenges versus dreaded sentences, which can propel them towards recovery.

Stagnating occurs when we lack the capacity to change our perceptions of life experiences. When people cling to pain they punish themselves, for anguish consumes energy and destroys creativity.

Therapists sometimes encounter clients who feel stagnant and are numbed, dazed, shocked, lifeless, and/or desensitized.

CATCHING AND CASTING ACTIONS

Emy's Story

I first came across the idea of reframing when taking courses in marriage and family therapy. The concept involves opening yourself to the possibility of different answers or explanations in a particular situation, one to which you thought you already had the answers or explanations. Using reframing in my personal life happened throughout the 1990s. When diagnosed with breast cancer, I came to understand that this was a wake up call for me. My initial reactions on hearing the news were shock, numbness, and deadness. Instead of taking my health for granted, which was the scene for some sixty years, there was a need now to set new priorities, conserve energies, limit social interactions, and discover outlets for release. I learned the hard way, through trial and error, that everyone has the freedom to make choices in life. I was the one who could select alternative responses, deciding to be happy or sad, to live in the moment or wait for the future. I became better at reframing crisis situations and shared my course of actions with friends. Upon examining past experiences I saw that hurts could include physical, mental, social, or emotional harm. In so doing, I found myself surviving bodily injuries, gaining from momentary lapses of the mind, becoming more compassionate with others due to losses, and having a better balanced existence due to distress. *Eventually my responses to pain did change. I could be more courageous after grief, laugh after despair, discover light in the darkest situations, and be hopeful in the very bleakest moments.*

I began sharing this reframing concept professionally with team members. I noted that times of pain, when we tend to be despondent, could be opportune moments to grow. When members relayed happenings in their lives such as failing an exam, having a project or paper rejected, or being scorned by associates, I suggested that they try reframing experiences. The process could involve seeing many sides of a situation, weighing both limits and possibilities, then deciding on a course of action to take. Since students wanted to further develop themselves, they accepted the challenge to alter their own perceptions and expand their own response sets to life experiences. Instead of viewing these times as wasted efforts, they came to conceive of them as future possibilities.

CATCHING AND RECASTING ACTIONS

Jennifer's Story

Have you ever moved into a new city and wanted to retreat from, rather than enter into, new friendships? Have you ever felt like running away from unfamiliar people in social situations instead of interacting with them? Growing up, my family relocated several times across the country. Often, in order to cope with the change, I withdrew from contacts. I avoided situations and probably made transitioning more difficult. Eventually, I began to realize that there had to be better ways to deal with tough times.

Being an engineering student at Purdue poses many challenges for most students. Some students happen to experience greater challenges than others. I was a struggling second year engineering student and staff member for the Undergraduate Mentoring Program when the concept of "reframing" was introduced to me by the Program Administrator, Dr. Emily Wadsworth. Emy told me that reframing was a way of coping with the countless academic obstacles

I was facing in the way of exams, course assignments, and projects. For me, the turning point in coping with these obstacles came about as a result of reframing certain happenings.

I had just learned, as a result of a poor grade, that I needed to re-take a particularly important but extremely difficult class for under-graduate majors in Mechanical Engineering. I was devastated! It wasn't that I hadn't studied and tried my hardest—it was that I just couldn't grasp the concepts. Emy encouraged me to rethink this event. She challenged me to view failure as an opportunity to grow versus as an ending to my college career. She told me of a way to turn this devas-tating, negative experience into a powerful, positive one—if only I could reframe the situation. In the future, she said, I might have greater confidence in my ability to face failure and conquer difficulties.

As it turned out, I did reframe my failure and was able to move through the class a second time with a positive attitude. I ended the course with an excellent grade and with a valuable experience to share with students who might face similar situations during their college careers.

At weekly team gatherings and monthly program meetings, I spoke with students who were struggling with classes and who were discouraged. I suggested that they reframe their difficulties and con-sider positive steps like taking advantage of tutors and study groups to improve their grades. I wanted my peers to persist and not give up. Through supporting program participants over the course of three years, I feel that I did my part to positively impact our program goal of retaining more undergraduate female engineering students.

After graduation, when I worked for a short time at Delco Electronics, I was assigned a project that needed a significant amount of attention and initiative to get off the ground. Other co-workers had attempted to start the project moving, but they had failed due to lack of vision. I spent my first days there trying to come up with ways to get the project going. I could easily have stagnated by turning the project back in and saying it was too difficult with my limited professional experience. Instead, I altered my thinking, knowing that if I could view this as an opportunity for professional growth and dig my heels in, the project would succeed.

I did reframe this "dead-end" project and searched for alternative solutions. To me, the answer lay in forming a team to pursue and maintain the upcoming technology challenges related to the project. I presented the problem and a solution for the project to the corporate technology team. They received my commendations openly. Then they created a team and told the group to follow through to completion. Therefore, by openly recognizing the potential and opportunity in a difficult project, I was able to bring about a corporate initiative.

Later at Delco, my workplace existence had become increasingly difficult. I again needed to alter my perceptions, this time related to one of my coworkers. This particular person exhibited aggressive behavior toward many people in the office. Her individual interactions with me were certainly much more negative than positive. By changing my attitude I was able to remove the control this individual had over my work experiences. Eventually, I became more adept at dealing with aggressive behaviors of people.

My experiences were quite different at a private specialized consulting firm where I was the only female engineer among nearly one hundred engineers and technicians. Difficulties relating to the cultural norms in a very conservative part of the country inevitably caused conflicts between the males and myself. I did try to reframe the situation to grow professionally and personally. However, working in this adverse environment with no guidance ended in stagnation. In order to overcome these feelings, I needed professional support and mentoring. In the absence of such, I chose to remove myself from this workplace and chalk it all up to a learning experience.

Years later, reframing played a vital role in coping with a personal crisis. The excitement and joy of a much-anticipated second child suddenly plummeted upon the news that I had undergone a late miscarriage. The incredible sadness and emotional devastation along with the physical recovery were almost beyond what I could bear. However, with the support of family, friends, and faith, my husband and I were able to change our perspective and attitudes towards this situation. In our minds, life itself became more precious. Each day, we learned to express our gratitude for everything that we have been given. I found that I could eventually reach out and administer to others undergoing personal recoveries from miscarriages.

The process of reframing is difficult to undertake, however, making use of it can quickly turn a stagnant attitude into the thought that life brings us many opportunities for personal and professional growth.

JENNIFER WENGER KING was awarded in 1996 a BS degree in Mechanical Engineering at Purdue University. She then accepted a position at Delco Electronics as a technical sales engineer. Now, she is married to Brian King, who graduated with an MS degree in Civil Engineering from Purdue and works for Procter & Gamble Corporation. Currently, Jennifer is a stay-at-home mother caring for two preschool age sons while expecting a third child. She mentors groups within the community where she lives.

Eight

Letting Go/Holding Tight

MEANINGS

Letting go involves releasing one's own fears and allowing what will be to be. When we let go we relinquish the need to control others. We start doing more accepting and focus our energies on establishing, maintaining, and conserving our human relationships. We fear less and live more. We accept "Thy will be done."

Holding tight involves clutching one's own fears closely and not having the self confidence to share thereby depriving others of contact with the real you. When we hold tight we strain to secure and consume. We tend to be angry, greedy, destructive, and dominating in relationships. We retain disappointments, bitterness, and blame. Such a person could be a daughter who remained angry with other family members all her life because of one happening . . . when their grandmother willed to another person and not to her the yellow cookie jar she thought she should receive.

CATCHING AND CASTING ACTIONS

Emy's Story

As our immediate family moved from New York to Indiana, back to New York, out to Oregon, and once again to Indiana, we had to let go of family and dear friends. When we first left New York State, it was heart wrenching to depart from a community of extended kin, including grandparents, parents, siblings, aunts, uncles, and cousins. We soon grasped that friends in Indiana would become our substitute for family. Each time we left one setting and moved on to another, we had to swallow our fears, reach out to others, test the waters, and initiate new relationships. Also, we were changing. We were not the same people returning to Indiana who had left years before. We had to be flexible and try to be patient with one another, for we were altering our ways of living. Over time there was less bickering, repudiating, condemning, and stagnating, among family members and we became more welcoming, trusting, and accepting. As we allowed ourselves and others the time to grow, we came closer to being the people we wanted to be.

During weekly meetings with female engineering students, *I discussed difficulties in letting go of the idea of possessing in human relationships and focusing instead on the concept of becoming.* We all realized that when we held tight and tried to dominate another, relationships would end. However, we also acknowledged that repenting, changing, and rebuilding connections with others takes time and energy. As students graduated and went on to professional careers and personal commitments, team members and I also had to learn to let go. At the same time, I wanted everyone involved with the programs to know that I felt gratitude for the years that we had together, appreciated being a part of their lives, and believed that they would go forth and be successful. This combination of action, feeling, and

belief helped the role transitions of students from being that of protégées to becoming colleagues. The receding or leaving to move on
with their existence, then the returning or coming back in later years
to be program speakers resembled the natural ebb and flow of relationships and life.

CATCHING AND RECASTING ACTIONS

Sabrina's Story

We all have had instances in life where we have held tight to things
and also many times where we've had to let go of things. Early in my
life, I held tight to my dreams and to my quest to do something great.
In the process, I met obstacles that presented stumbling blocks and
distractions. Those were the things that I let go. Later in life, as I met
with greater and more substantial challenges, I discovered that I
began to hold onto the very things that I needed to let go. I also let go,
all too easily, the very things that I needed to hold on to. The truth be
told, these pages describing my personal experiences at Purdue University are evidence of the very beginning of my letting go.

When I began my graduate studies at Purdue, I left a very small
and supportive environment at my undergraduate institution and at
the church that I attended throughout my undergraduate years on
the East Coast. I left behind family members who lived nearby and
many people who had become surrogate family members who offered support, encouragement, and strength to my husband and me.
Moving to the Midwest, to Purdue, was quite an event for me. During
my adjustment to the large and less diverse environment, I held
tightly to my husband, many memories of and communications with
loved ones from our undergraduate years, and to previous successes
and triumphs. Burdened with the fear of making a transition from a

small university where I majored in chemistry to a large engineering program at Purdue, I felt somewhat intimidated and insecure. I began my graduate study with reluctance and a hesitation—probably a common response to facing something unknown and uncertain. I went through periods where disappointments developed in academics and in my personal life and I began to cling instead to the growing resentment that stemmed from losing the comfort and familiarity of the former supportive environment of my undergraduate years.

My involvement with the Mentoring Program for Women in Engineering started when I became a participant. I recall that the monthly meetings were designed to facilitate interaction between participants/peers and also between a mentee and her mentor. Each program meeting began with an icebreaker that helped us to open up to one another. Each month, staff members assigned participants to a dinner table so that they could sit with different people whom they might otherwise not have seen or met on campus. Female faculty members who were program guests attended meetings regularly and they often added insightful comments to conversations that took place before and after scheduled speakers. Together, all present had opportunities to share and celebrate successes as well as concerns in this group setting. I began to feel more at ease knowing that there were others around me who had fears and disappointments like the ones I experienced. Holding on to my fears and resentment, however, prevented me from truly selfless loving, accepting others, and opening up.

When I became a staff member for the Graduate Mentoring Program, I attended weekly team meetings that began with a warm up planned by the meeting facilitator. At times we shared personal details about ourselves, from our inspirations in life to our favorite colors. These activities helped to begin our planning meetings with a sense of openness. Having a feeling of familiarity with one another enabled team members to both offer and accept suggestions and/or criticisms about ideas surfacing through discussions. Similarly, this openness allowed staff members to communicate effectively about problems encountered or assistance needed with individual responsibilities.

As a staff member, I recall that our Program Administrator, Dr. Emily Wadsworth, discussed with us that it takes time and energy to build human relationships. She suggested that our members gather outside of team meetings in order to strengthen our bonds as a group. Emy sponsored get-togethers for staff members apart from our regular weekly meetings so that we could interact on a more personal and social level. Right before team members graduated, we had events where we acknowledged their contributions to our program and their progressions to professional positions. We realized that our relationships could advance to another level as staff moved on into the operational world.

The interconnections among participants and staff members afforded many an opportunity to grow from letting go and holding tight. Monthly meeting activities were very well planned to help persons like myself let go of fears and disappointments. Sharing successes and failures alike strengthened the bonds between participants. For example, knowing that a small army of supportive women is quietly cheering you on during your preliminary examination or dissertation defense can be quite comforting. Knowing that the same small army of women will be there to show acceptance regardless of the outcome can also be comforting. This type of support served as a strong anchor onto which many students held during their course of study in graduate school. As with any relationship, however, participants also had to let go of each other at the end of their studies. To help facilitate this process, the program group celebrated big events and milestones in the lives of participants. Through these celebrations, we learned about both the personal and professional endeavors of participants.

In some cases, graduates returned to campus or corresponded with us as a means of sharing their successes after graduating.

Although I was in the center of a group of people who had at least one common struggle, namely being a female engineering graduate student, I was not receiving the full benefit that such a wonderful group could offer. My focus continued to remain on my disappointments and "what could have been" instead of the positives before me. I engaged in casual conversation and showed genuine happiness with other people's successes and genuine sadness with their failures. I did not, however, share my own ups and downs, concerns, fears, or shortcomings. Thinking about or sharing such things were difficult for me then because I thought of my setbacks as failures and evidence of weakness. My tenure as a program participant and as a staff member was very helpful to me in terms of gaining strategies and experiences that would help me to succeed in life, but I walked away with few deep and lasting friendships from the group. I tremendously enjoyed the time that I spent working with my colleagues and helping wherever I could, but my "busyness" served mainly as a temporary distraction to my "holding on" to my fears and disappointments. My colleagues at school, as a result, did not get to know the real me and I deprived myself of opportunities to grow and establish meaningful relationships that would have provided the very support, acceptance, and validation that I needed in school.

Toward the end of my graduate studies, I began to feel the isolation that my actions created. Solid, lasting relationships can only be built on a foundation of truth—something that I was not extending to others. Upon the completion of my doctorate degree, I set out again, this time on my own, leaving behind everything familiar (church, family, and even my husband while he finished his degree) to chart unknown territories and to do some introspective thinking. Away from the school environment, I was able to take some time to reflect on my existence and the paths that I had taken over my life. In solitude, I realized why I did not allow others to see the real me.

I had a similar start when beginning my professional career as I had in beginning graduate school. I made myself available to help others and did not acknowledge my own needs. Within the first several months of work and after becoming less fearful, I became more open to establishing, maintaining, and conserving my relationships. It has been a gradual process that is still not yet complete.

In my work relationships, I am now better at letting go of my fears of failure on projects. I have opened up to colleagues and have begun sharing my plans and my ideas for which I also invite criticism. I seek to establish new relationships with my colleagues, letting go of my fear of rejection or disapproval. In the process, I am finding great comfort in discovering that I have more positive encounters than negative ones. I am letting go of my habit of not asking for what I feel I need for success. I am learning how compensating for team members who do not perform can be a detriment to me and to team progress. With a more assertive attitude, I now recognize that my compensating was actually a missed opportunity to provide constructive criticism to a team member that could help that team member's personal and professional development as well as assist the team in succeeding.

In my current mentoring roles on the job as well as in after school programs, I still face the challenge of holding on to the things that I should readily let go of. Unrealized expectations and fears of criticism still surface and provoke my withdrawal. I am still somewhat hesitant to share my experiences and open up.

I have learned, however, that true growth is achieved through continued attempts in spite of failures. Through examining my motives and acknowledging and owning and expressing my needs, I have become a much more assertive person. I am less fearful of people seeing the "real me" and as a result I have deeper and much more meaningful relationships with my family and friends both old and new.

SABRINA HOOD MYRICK was awarded a BS degree in Chemistry at Norfolk State University in 1993, an MS degree in Chemical Engineering at Purdue University in 1993, and a PhD in Chemical Engineering at Purdue University in 1999. She then accepted a position with E.I. DuPont de Nemours and Company as a Senior Engineer in Lycra® Research and Development and subsequently as a Chemist and Dispersion Process Engineer for the DuPont Performance Coatings Group. She met and married Wilbur L. Myrick at Norfolk State where they both obtained their undergraduate degrees. Wilbur was awarded MS and PhD degrees in Electrical Engineering at Purdue University. He is currently a Research and Development Engineer with SAIC (Science Applications International Company).

Nine

Rejoicing/Grieving

MEANINGS

Rejoicing has to do with feeling great joy and delight. Celebrating, reveling, thanking, succeeding, exulting, fulfilling, can all be related to rejoicing. Births, graduations, promotions, weddings, and anniversaries can be events that involve rejoicing.

Grieving means feeling deep sorrow and distress. Suffering, melancholy, emptiness, grumbling, and mourning can all be associated with grieving. Feelings of guilt for possibly causing a breakup of a marital relationship or for not spending more quality time with children can rise to the surface during grieving times.

CATCHING AND CASTING ACTIONS

Emy's Story

Personally, my knowledge concerning grieving was gained during the two years that our daughter was in a coma and afterwards when she died. I experienced first hand the gut wrenching feeling of deep sorrow, painful anguish, and intense suffering that accompanies the loss of a loved one, especially a child. It was hard to focus on anything outside myself when passing through periods of denial, anger, blame, guilt, fear, and remorse. I asked out loud many times *why?* Why did this happen, why Mary, why this young woman and not me? I wondered *how?* How to let her go and cope with the grieving process? I thought *what?* What to do in order to adapt and recover from this situation? Right away I wanted to comprehend all of life, know why things happened when they did, why things were meant to be. It took time for me to acknowledge that death is mysterious and complex. I became comfortable with the fact that there are many unknowns. I stopped groping for the answers to *why?* Instead, there emerged a personal view of the grieving process as a series of stages that can include shock, emptiness, commitment, and recovery. I slowed down and gave myself time to work through these stages and reach some resolution to *how.* A decision was made on my part to seek empathy, comfort, and compassion within a small group of women who started on a Spiritual Journey and this helped me with *what* to do. We three mourned, read, lamented, searched, discussed, celebrated, thanked, exalted, really came to terms with and triumphed over our human difficulties.

Professionally, I relayed my personal experiences concerning grieving and rejoicing with team members when they asked me to talk about death and life. They heard about my near death experience, from which I learned that death is peaceful and not to be feared, and from which an assurance came to me that there is life after our time on earth. I shared my readings on bereavement that indicated most people move from grief to recovery in two or three years after the death of a loved one. The process usually involves several succeeding stages: separation from the deceased; some withdrawal from human contact; a search for the meaning of death; a disorganization of one's present life; greater involvement with other people; and finally a reorganization for one's life in the future. My own recovery after my daughter's death was advanced through honoring special past moments involving her, like an annual Santa Lucia Celebration on December 13 when she would prepare a breakfast for our family to mark the start of holiday festivities. Close relationships with concerned family members, friends, and associates also helped. *It is through such heartaches, healings, and human connections that we can come to understand that grieving, darkness, is linked with rejoicing, lightness.*

CATCHING AND RECASTING ACTIONS

Tracy's Story

Thus far in my life I have encountered events related to rejoicing and events related to grieving.

The joyous times have included completion of engineering degrees, a wonderful marriage, a successful career, and the birth of two children. When I finished six years of higher education I felt proud that I had accomplished such an enormous goal. When I dated John and later when we were married, I realized how fortunate I was to find such a caring and loving mate with whom I could share my life. When I was hired by Arvin Industries I was apprehensive at first, but then became confident in my ability to perform competently on the job. When my children were born healthy and whole I was so grateful for the beautiful blessings I had been given.

Unfortunately, life does not come without its share of sorrow. I have experienced grieving related to the divorce of my parents, the death of my grandparents, the dissolution of close personal relationships, and the decision to put my career indefinitely "on hold" to stay at home and raise my children. When my parents divorced I felt like my family was being bitterly torn apart and I experienced guilt for having to choose to live with one parent over another. When my grandparents died I wondered why they didn't get more happy "golden years" to live. When personal relationships ended I was grief stricken and felt like I had failed. When I was trying to make the decision to continue with or put a hold on my career, I struggled with giving up the self-satisfaction that I received from my professional career.

I believe that the joys we receive in life help us to cope with the struggles and persist through difficult events in search of happier times.

One of my experiences with rejoicing occurred during my college years at a weekly session for staff members of the Undergraduate Mentoring Program. Our Program Administrator, Dr. Emily Wadsworth, regularly discussed how important it was to rejoice in life's gifts. I remember one team meeting specifically that was extremely significant in teaching me a valuable life lesson. Emy opened this fall meeting by passing out to each of us some colorful sugar maple leaves that she had picked up on her walk to the Civil Engineering Building. Her beaming smile and the wonder in her eyes communicated to all present how much she enjoyed the little things in life and how capturing daily moments enriched her entire existence. She taught us that we shouldn't take the world's beauty for granted and she encouraged us to take time out to appreciate all that we had been given.

Dr. Wadsworth often signed personal correspondence "Catch the Joy as it Flies!" I think this simple statement communicated a very profound message. It reminded us to keep our eyes open so that we may recognize the joys in life and capture those times and memories in order to relish them fully.

I know the gift our administrator had for cherishing all things was a true learning and mentoring experience for me as well as other team members. Emy taught me to step back from situations and problems, to look at the bigger picture, and to be thankful for the relationships and gifts I have been given.

While involved in the M&M Program at Purdue University, the program participants shared their rejoicing and grieving experiences at monthly meeting times where students related happenings in their collegiate lives. Some specific examples of rejoicing and grieving expressed were delight in passing a difficult exam, concern with personal academic performance, satisfaction in receiving an internship job offer, and anxiety relating to interviewing for a summer job.

Increasing the retention rates for undergraduate female engineering students was the goal of the M&M Program. Rejoicing greatly impacted this primary goal. Monthly meeting sharing times were crucial in allowing participants to connect with staff members and other participants of the M&M Program. At these gatherings we affirmed the progress of participants (e.g., completing a class project, passing a difficult course, receiving a corporate scholarship) and encouraged them to persist with their studies. Through these actions students would feel good about their progress and hopefully "hang in there" until they obtained their engineering degrees.

I show appreciation for my life every day. As a mother, I rejoice in the little as well as the big victories and accomplishments while caring for my daughter and son. Watching my children interact with their world, I am amazed at the wonder and delight they find in new experiences. The world moves more slowly for children . . . they take time to appreciate . . . they find joy in little things. I wish we could all remember how we learned as children when we turn into busy adults with too much to do and too little time for counting important blessings in life.

I found it extremely important to also rejoice in professional victories. Being a past leader of a product launch team with over 30 team members, I tried to emphasize how crucial it was to praise, celebrate, and congratulate our team's accomplishments. I think this practice fostered respect among team members and enabled us to take pride in a job well done. The product launch was an incredible success and some bonds formed among team members professionally and personally that will last a lifetime.

During my transition from college to the workplace, I experienced grieving over saying goodbye to very close friends and team members. I knew the friendships and bonds that were formed between us would forever change. The uncertainty of how the connections would be sustained throughout distance and time concerned me. The anxiety regarding the waiting working world only compounded the situation, making it harder for me to cope. I recall Emy talking about her sadness when her only daughter died. When staff members questioned her about death, she shared a story she had written about her own near-death experience. She discussed steps she had taken which enabled her to move forward and gain from the pain of this event.

Leaving college experiences and close personal relationships behind was difficult yet inevitable. However, I realized the time had come to move on to another stage in my life. I knew that if I wanted to maintain these friendships, I was responsible for dedicating the time and effort needed in order to keep in contact. Also, I tried to be optimistic and excited about my new career and the role it would play in my life. These transitions proved to be difficult, but the results were rewarding. I am fortunate that my career has thus far been very successful and, more importantly, that my close friendships have survived distance and time. I revel in my career accomplishments and I am extremely grateful for my close friends.

Although there have been challenges involved with moving

forward to yet another phase in my life, that of being an at-home mother, and even though at times days can be difficult, from the darkness comes the light, like a rainbow after the storm.

TRACY RICHMOND-SCHOSTEK received both her BS and MS degrees in Industrial Engineering from Purdue University, respectively in 1992 and 1994. She has worked these past seven years at Arvin Industries in engineering and program management. She is married to John Schostek, also a Purdue engineering graduate, who is now an operations manager for Ingersoll-Rand. Tracy and John have two preschool-age children.

Ten

Balancing/Tilting

MEANINGS

Balancing occurs when we achieve harmony between various parts of our existence at home, at work, and in the community, which involves time spent with mate, children, parents, other family members, and friends. When we acquire balance in our lives we can enjoy a sense of equilibrium, steadiness, and stability. Balance is something we continually need to check on since once attained it is not necessarily kept. This means we evaluate and reevaluate our priorities and rearrange our lives over time.

Tilting occurs when we lack balance between the various parts of our existence. When we are unbalanced in living we may have a sense of being slanted, biased, tilted toward one or another aspect of our life. This could happen when we repeatedly spend sixteen hours a day working and end up with little or no quality time with a mate, children, or friends.

CATCHING AND CASTING ACTIONS

Emy's Story

Most of my life I have followed the ethic of work first, then play later. Since I tended to take life very seriously and was a workaholic, this left little time for quality play. It has only been in the last decade, after the death of our daughter and my own breast cancer, that a balance between daily exertion and daily leisure has been obtained. I have been forced to rest and care for myself in order to tend to my loved ones and have finally given myself permission to relax. Even though it is very difficult for me, I have sought and found pleasurable moments. To me, leisure is free, unforced, unoccupied time to recreate, to discover inner resources, to focus on what has been given rather than what is lacking, to see the cup half full instead of half empty. *When we are at leisure we can be open, fluid, creative. We can laugh and be joyful. We can fill ourselves up so that we can then give forth to others.* During these retirement years, my husband and I have become more assertive as to where to put our time and energies. We balance hours of leisure with hours of labor. We desire more spontaneity and less scheduling. We want to let each other be rather than making each other do. We take time off, enjoying monthly mini-breaks such as an evening concert or a weekend away, and yearly maxi-vacations that can last several weeks. The result is that instead of having an existence that is terrifically fast-paced, distorted, and tilted towards drudgery, grind, and stress, we have a life that is slower-paced, leveled, composed, and oriented toward lightness, creativity, and pure pleasure.

When transferring the above principles to my professional administrator duties, I still expected team members to complete weekly and monthly tasks related to the mentoring programs. This was the only way the programs could survive. Yet I also wanted student leaders to experience fun in their work. As a result, during weekly meetings we talked about movies and sports events we saw, books we read, cartoons we enjoyed, and many happy weekend moments. We celebrated birthdays, job offers, and engagements. I wanted these women to appreciate their existence, to learn about their differences, to acknowledge their growth in life, to be confident about their going forth, and to invest in human relationships. I hoped that they would find resting and relaxing in their personal lives as important as working and succeeding in their professional lives.

CATCHING AND RECASTING ACTIONS

Robin's Story

While working as a consulting engineer prior to graduate school, my life was definitely tilted toward professional endeavors. In the two consulting firms where I worked, I was the only female engineer in a small office, and the only engineer with a degree from a midwestern university. This situation did not lend itself well to developing social relationships with coworkers.

When I first relocated to a new city, I tried hard to find fulfillment outside of the office. Unfortunately it was difficult for me to locate organizations or groups that offered friendships and opportunities outside of the workplace. I looked into countless activities to expand my social horizons but always without much luck. I joined a church, and while I met some interesting people of like mind, I never found individuals with whom I could socialize. I tried various sporting activities from volleyball to cross country skiing and it would seem just as I located someone to connect with, they wouldn't come back the following weeks. Seemingly, every activity I wanted to be a part of was already a closed circle offering little for outsiders. The fact that I am reserved, and initially uncomfortable in new situations, made it harder for me (although friends who know me find this hard to believe).

Because I didn't find outside fulfillment, I spent a lot of time on or at my profession. I would go to the office on Saturdays to work and then take work home at night. When deadlines would approach, I would labor all night at home in order to complete a project. With each new challenge, I found my life strongly tilted to work with little escape except for the television and long distance phone calls to family and friends.

I returned to Purdue University in 1993 to pursue a master's degree in Civil Engineering, but I was not a typical graduate student due to my age and experience. I was several years older than most of my colleagues, which gave me a different perspective. I received my BS from Purdue in 1986, obtained my professional engineering license in 1990, and worked as a consulting structural engineer for several years prior to returning to school full time. Although there was course work that some would have considered "required," I knew from my work experience that certain courses would not be of great benefit for me in my consulting career. These classes I took less seriously, without concern for the instructor's perception of my talents or of the final grade I would receive. I started taking time to make new friends in classes and to play soccer and softball. Although I wasn't good at either sport, I enjoyed both.

When I was invited by Dr. Emily Wadsworth to become a staff member for the Graduate Mentoring Program, I was beginning to find a balance between academics and the rest of my life. The M&M Program helped me to maintain this stability. During weekly meetings with Emy and the other members of our staff we would talk about our activities and things we might do together as a leadership team. We got together for nights out and even had a cookout at my parent's house. Although I was an older student, I had swallowed my pride and moved back home with my retired parents in order to be able to afford graduate school. During these times together we talked about school, careers, the M&M program and other issues relevant to our lives.

Our monthly group meetings were not solely focused on school or academic related issues. We would have icebreakers at the beginning of each gathering, which facilitated our getting to know one another and our feeling comfortable as a group. These activities also helped us in making new friends with whom we could share struggles, concerns, and achievements. This in turn balanced difficulties involved with being in graduate school. These meetings also provided diverse information for students including career planning and health issues.

We would host practicing female engineers who would discuss the struggles and rewards they faced in their professional and personal lives and how they had achieved and maintained balance. These professionals included engineers employed in industry, government laboratories, and universities and they became needed role models. The women offered us the chance to see how we might shape our futures and accomplish many things we wanted to do while achieving desired balance in our living.

We had female speakers with doctorates in nutrition and health address us on the importance of daily diets and exercise. They gave tips on good foods to eat and places to go for physical conditioning. They also supplied information on stress management and its related health issues.

Creating meetings that had fun activities, that presented a variety of issues, and that had credible speakers from various fields of study were all means of assisting participants in sustaining balance and remaining in advanced degree programs. In these ways, the M&M Program helped increase the number of engineering graduate degrees for females at our institution.

I was fortunate upon graduation to already have a job lined up. I sent out very few letters of interest and had just one interview, in Orlando. That one interview sealed the job for me. I ended up with a position in a new city with new challenges to face. Although there were two other women engineers at this office, they were in different departments and we had little interaction on the job. Once again I found myself in a male-dominated environment with little in my life to balance work. I labored on Saturdays and Sundays as needed to help a financially strapped department within our company meet deadlines and achieve economic stability. During my second year with this company, I met my future husband. A friend from work introduced us and after a short period of time we were spending most of our free hours together.

During this same period, my boss, who was one of the principals of the company, called our entire department together to talk about financial difficulties. Part of the discussion concerned our responsibilities to the company. It was stated that we would need to do whatever was required to turn the department around economically. We were told that we would be asked and expected to put in 50, 60, or 70 plus hours a week to achieve success. I asked, "What about our other obligations outside of the office, our families, etc.?" I was told, "Don't let the CEO hear you talking like that, this department should be your priority."

At that point I knew there were larger issues at hand. My future husband had a 6-year-old son, for whom he had responsibility every other weekend. These two people were now my priority. We spent weekends when we were together doing things as a "family." We would go bike riding, roller-blading, or swimming in the pool at my apartment complex. I had found personal balance, but this balance was now threatening my career.

After about a year of dating my husband to be, I found out that I was being passed over for a position as an associate at the company. Male engineers who had been there less time than I were given the title and all the privileges of associate status. In a discussion with my boss, I found out that I was not considered for associate because I "had other priorities." That was a hard pill to swallow. I had helped this company with a huge engineering problem created by a previous employee. I had spent numerous hours coming up with engineering solutions, resolving problems, and stressing over havoc created by someone else. Seemingly, my contributions were not sufficient for my promotion to associate. It was explained to me that other engineers in our area had picked up the slack because I had to concentrate on this problem project. My boss made it clear that other employees, all males, were a priority for him. He did not want them to feel slighted because of the attention I was receiving for helping the company out of a difficult situation.

By the summer of 1997, I felt I had found a balance between my career and personal life. However, my employer felt differently despite my efforts on their behalf. They felt that my life was "tilted" toward my family. It was at this point that my feelings shifted. I was no longer happy doing engineering, because I felt like I was getting the short end of the stick. I went to work every morning but did not enjoy the challenges in which I had previously found pleasure. The company's attitude toward me had changed my entire attitude towards engineering. I was ready to quit it all and flip hamburgers or bag groceries. But as is often said, "timing is everything."

I put in a phone call to an engineering friend and told him that if he knew of anyone who was looking for a structural engineer, to please give them my name. Within two days, I received a call from this friend letting me know that a gentleman at a major entertainment company in Orlando (I will let you draw your own conclusions) was expecting a call from me. I phoned immediately and spoke with the man who would soon become my supervisor.

Within five days the chance for a better balance in my life occurred. I accepted an offer as a structural engineer with an entertainment giant and gave my notice to the company that originally brought me to Orlando. After eight months in my new job, my husband and I became engaged and harmony between my personal and professional existence was achieved and has continued to flourish.

My new engineering position has provided challenges I never expected, although it isn't rocket science. I am willing to work any hour of the day doing all types of structural engineering and forensics. I enjoy the opportunity to work third shift performing investigations when they arise because I know that I can be with my family when needed. My now 11-year-old stepson and husband are my focus. My current supervisor understands family commitments. Since he and I are part of a family-based entertainment corporation, he knows that I will go the extra mile to help out the company and its various divisions. I have come in frequently at 11 P.M. or 5 A.M. to do work after or before hours in order to meet operation requirements. When I put that extra effort into my engineering position, my supervisor is receptive to flexibility in my work hours. I can then spend time with my husband and stepson. Finally, I have truly achieved balance with my career and my family life.

ROBIN SEIBERT SCHININA, P.E., was awarded BS and MS degrees in Civil Engineering at Purdue University respectively in 1986 and 1995. In 1996 she met her husband, Jim, who is a Director of Marketing for Perfection Architectural Systems in Winter Park, Florida. Robin is a Senior Structural Engineer with a large entertainment company in Orlando, Florida.

Eleven

Focusing/Blurring

MEANINGS

Focusing involves centering and reflecting on one's life. Focusing requires taking time to be still, to explore, to analyze and consider one's life, thereby becoming aware of patterns and progressions. Some senior citizens have spent a few of their retirement years writing and distributing their memoirs. These books can illustrate a growing awareness over time of the interrelatedness of one's body, mind, heart, and soul.

Blurring involves bewilderment and confusion about one's life. Blurring occurs if I do not take time to consider why am I here and what am I doing. In such a situation people can be unwilling to initiate any changes in their existence.

CATCHING AND CASTING ACTIONS

Emy's Story

From my near death experience came the belief that my inner essence, my essential being, is what proceeds on to eternity. I *finally had grasped the value of centering, being still, finding repose. Such moments helped me focus, evaluate, and prioritize.* Rising early in the morning gave me a wonderful hour of solitude. I desperately needed these quiet times to sustain me and provide my life with a sense of direction. I read a variety of publications, started journaling, and concentrated on where I had come from and where I was going. The result was a heightened awareness of the negative or dark aspects along with the positive or light aspects of existence. Negative, dark aspects include our fears, anger, sorrows, sicknesses, and death, while positive, light aspects include peace, love, joy, health, and life. The challenge was to resolve and decrease the dark sides of my being while acknowledging and increasing the light sides of my existence. Questions surfaced in my mind: What do I fear? What do I long for in life? What brings me joy? What would make my life more complete? I thought about each question and wrote down a set of responses over several months. Finally, I focused on what had happened in my life, trying to understand the way in which different experiences had interacted to establish the unique creation that was *me!* My detaching, going inward, had strengthened me to then attach and proceed outward.

In my professional life I have worked with many students in different universities. Some of the most rewarding moments have been when just two of us have come together to get away from the fast-paced, frantic churning in our lives, to talk about a problem or disturbing situation. On these occasions we have focused . . . centered . . . stilled ourselves. We have shared our fears, angers, sorrows, and sicknesses and stated our longings for peace, love, joy, and health. We have made ourselves vulnerable in an attempt to connect deeply with one another . . . to more completely comprehend each other. Later, these former students would send cards, notes, letters, or poems that made me realize they were in fact focusing in their lives and concentrating on their inner essence. I was delighted for them and recalled how the pattern of my life had become interlaced with the patterns of their lives. Jointly we had accepted existing in a larger whole, reached mutual understandings, strengthened each other's lives, taken an inner direction, and discovered a sense of peace in order to exist in an outer world and prepare ourselves for a world beyond this world.

CATCHING AND RECASTING ACTIONS

Anne's Story

Twelve years. I think back and it is a collage of memories, thoughts, feelings and learnings. The academics were rigorous. The life lessons were even more so. It was a time of self-discovery and re-creation. My years at Purdue have some of my fondest memories and some of the most painful. I moved from adolescence into adulthood with all the accompanying pain and joy.

As I look back, I can appreciate all the experiences, the lessons that I learned, and the paths down which I trod. At the time, however, I often felt overwhelmed by life and what was demanded of me. I can remember so many times when the burdens were almost too much to bear. It was during these times that I learned the art of pouring out my thoughts on paper. I began to practice journaling— recording my thoughts and experiences in written form.

The act of writing allowed me to focus. All the conflicting thoughts and emotions, which at times seemed blurred, were captured on one piece of paper. The act itself allowed me to acknowledge and validate my thoughts. Rereading my entries became like looking in a mirror. This helped me to pause, reflect, and put things into proper perspective. Reading past journal entries brought me comfort because I was able to track my growth over time.

I found that gathering the myriad of emotions and thoughts on paper allowed me to analyze (important to an engineer) past conduct and prescribe future action. Instead of being paralyzed by emotion, I became energized by it. It also allowed me to quietly listen for and receive direction.

During my graduate years, I was asked to become first a participant and then a staff person for the Graduate Mentoring Program. This initiative was set up to support graduate women engineers. Along the way I met people who were walking a similar path of self-discovery. Interwoven with my journaling, I composed poems and shared copies with women who were connected with me through this program and through community organizations. One of these people was our Program Administrator—Dr. Emily Wadsworth. Emy affirmed me for my poetry and she appreciated my efforts at focusing. Through my roles as a mentee and mentor I discovered a powerful means to express my innermost thoughts and feelings with fellow female engineers.

I expanded journaling past the written and into the spoken word. As I mentored others, I recalled past events in order to empathize with a mentee's current situation. The reflection and focus was designed to expand the perspective of my mentee. More often than not, I gained greater perspective on my own life when disclosing to another person.

Many times a mentee would come to me overwhelmed either in her studies, interactions with professors, or personally. A blur of emotions was often overwhelming my mentee. I knew we would need to air the emotions and then move past the feelings to focus on the cause. Once focused on the cause, we were then better equipped to identify possible solutions. Seemingly hopeless situations often had very attainable solutions. Thus, what often felt like insurmountable challenges became the stepping-stones of accomplishments leading to a graduate degree.

Focusing helped me to remove the extraneous and distinguish elements essential to achieving my goals and realizing my dreams. Similarly, I was able to help my mentees, through focusing, to eliminate the clutter often associated with the daily frustrations of student life. Creating quiet moments in our daily lives helped us counterbalance the stress we were experiencing as graduate students. Likewise, being in a group with other female engineering students helped us to forge a bond, focus on tasks at hand, and keep on persevering until we obtained our graduate degrees.

After what seemed an eternity and at the same time a nanosecond, I received my PhD, and headed out into the "real world" for a "real job." With my husband still at Purdue, I moved to California and set up home and office.

The first few months were once again a whirlwind. I was excited then scared, enthusiastic then inundated, optimistic then overwhelmed, lonely then craving solitude. My journal provided a means once again to focus, record, reflect and receive direction.

It didn't take too long for me to overcome the newcomer status and settle right into my professional position. I was the mentee again. I relished the opportunity to receive guidance from those who had "been there, done that." Mentors introduced me to the hierarchy, sharing insights on "how to get things done" in my new world. I was in the "real world" now, a culture very different from academia. My new mentors are still helping to transition me through the culture shock.

I enjoy being a mentee even more now that I understand how much I am giving back to my mentors. I realize I am in the position of enabling others to focus, reflect, and regroup even as they share with me.

Currently, I am not part of a formal mentoring program. However, informal mentoring occurs at my workplace with colleagues.

Further, long distance mentoring takes place with former friends and associates. I hope to continue encouraging other women in engineering, recruiting them to join me in the challenging and very rewarding pursuit of engineering careers. I have discovered that mentoring occurs on many different levels, and while one who has experience and success in the industry may mentor me, I may mentor her in other ways.

I continue to learn life's lessons, which often come in unexpected ways, tangled in emotions, often at dizzying speeds. It is easy to let the events of the hour or day slip by in a blur. Along the way, I have learned to take time to focus on the day, the event or the situation. I find focusing brings clarity, insight, and purpose to the sometimes inexplicable combinations and often overwhelming experiences that make up life.

ANNE GICK was awarded BS, MS, and PhD degrees in Aeronautics and Astronautics at Purdue University respectively in 1991, 1994, and 1999. She then accepted a position as an engineer working on the GPS Disposal Orbit Stability Project for The Aerospace Corporation. She is married to Jon Gick, a Purdue Electrical Engineering Technology graduate, who recently joined Raytheon Electronic Systems in California. Anne and Jon's first child, a daughter, was born in May of 2002.

Twelve

Gracing/Alienating

MEANINGS

Gracing occurs when one receives unexpected gifts of insight. We do not seek grace; rather, grace seeks us. Grace is intangible, not easily defined or grasped. We can let others know that grace exists and is always waiting there for them.

Alienating occurs when one encounters estrangement. Withdrawal, detachment, loss, and unfriendliness, can all be associated with alienation. Hostility, torment, and revenge can also be involved. People who have suffered through broken romances, bitter separations and divorces, and who have had great difficulties raising rebellious children, know what alienating means.

CATCHING AND CASTING ACTIONS

Emy's Story

From childhood, many of us are socialized to play by the rules, get good grades, partake of activities, and make progress. We work hard to earn a living, buy a house, have a vacation. In return we yearn for praise, for gratitude, and for satisfaction. We *do* in order to *receive*. Yet I have come to believe that grace is a gift that can take the form of love, forgiveness, power, or understanding that comes from beyond ourselves and springs within ourselves. This belief can lead us to unconditionally love other people and be loved by them despite our defects, failures, and limits. If we live in grace then we will be able to respond with grace towards others. In such a situation, We *receive* just because we *are*. As a result of grace received through personal experiences with dying and death, I became transformed as a human being. Where once my behaviors could be termed critical, withdrawn, and revengeful, they were now more accepting, comforting, and compassionate. I concentrated on my potential for good versus evil. I "lightened up," lived in the present moment, and became conscious of receiving what I termed were daily serendipities, times of pure pleasure alone or with another human being. Such instances could be these: seeing a pod of spouting whales or brilliant hues in a summer sunset; listening to swing music or an ancient family story; smelling a fragrant English rose or freshly baked spice cookies; touching a cashmere scarf or warmly hugging a friend; tasting a fresh fruit tart or sipping a glass of aged red wine. I learned to catch the joy as it flies!

In my professional work, I have found that most students are reinforced for what they do instead of who they are. They would enter the university with high cognitive ability yet at critical times their self-esteem took a dive. When they failed an assignment or received a low exam grade, they felt they didn't have whatever it takes to make it in college and they wanted to withdraw from the field. In the hours spent talking individually or collectively with students, I relayed my insights on gracing and alienating attained throughout my own life. I told them about caring for and appreciating them not for what they did but just for who they were. I said that when we progress through periods of being alienated, when the life we longed for has not appeared, often these are times when gracing occurs. *I became conscious that words coming through me to them originated from an inner voice and they were far more creative and wiser than what my mind would normally generate. It was during these times I/WE experienced grace.*

CATCHING AND RECASTING ACTIONS

Linda's Story

Upon entering the Ph.D. program at Purdue, I had earned a master's degree and bachelor's degree in engineering from two different universities while maintaining perfect grades. Professionally, I was a bright star with great potential. Personally, I was struggling. At 18, I had married a young man. By 21, I was divorced. Throughout this trauma and in the ensuing years, I had attended college and studied voraciously. Academic achievement was my ticket to a secure future. My mother's words rang in my head: "Once you get a degree, nobody can take it away."

Sadly, I never took the time to grieve after the divorce. My personal development was not on course with my professional growth. Frankly, I never had the time. I worked constantly. My professors encouraged me at every juncture to pursue the next level. My relationships were sometimes rocky, but that didn't seem to affect my ability to excel in school. Remarkably, I achieved this success in engineering. This meant I was routinely the only female in class and all of my engineering professors were men. Relationships with females were rarely a part of my life.

Moving to the Midwest and enrolling in a top-five engineering graduate program was a new challenge. I felt that the professors I worked with were interested mostly in their own careers. Student personal growth seemed to be a distraction from "real" work in their competitive system. Because I challenged the status quo, I received little affirmation.

Shortly after enrolling, I received news that my mother had breast cancer. The threat of losing Mom shook me to the core. In my mind, I was accumulating college degrees as much for my parents as for me. I became despondent, and my male professors and colleagues were emotionally unavailable. One professor, after hearing my news of family illness, advised me to "throw myself into my work." I became depressed and nearly quit college.

My situation changed when I became one of five original staff members for the Engineering Graduate Mentoring Program. When I joined, I knew a great deal about alienating but little about gracing. I had learned about alienating on the receiving end—through being a young divorcee, having few female companions and role models, misunderstandings with graduate professors, and undergoing private torture over Mom's cancer. My experience with grace was paltry by comparison.

I began to meet weekly with the Program Administrator, Dr. Emily Wadsworth, and four other women engineering graduate students to plan the mentoring program. Once a month, about fifty graduate students just like me attended our monthly meetings. I began to receive grace through human connection. Dr. Wadsworth, Emy, had done her doctoral work in the area of human development. In contrast to our engineering work with equipment and equations, she taught us subjects like team dynamics, leadership development, and conflict resolution. In this new world, it was okay to have emotions. I want to emphasize how novel this concept was; engineers generally stress hard facts and figures and are uneasy with so-called "soft" topics. Being allowed to feel the depth of my emotions was a grace—an unexpected gift—which sharply contradicted the messages of engineering life.

I gradually began to open up and trust people in the program. During one early staff meeting, Emy quietly told us she had been diagnosed with breast cancer. I could not hide my terror. I calmly finished the meeting. A few days later, I began to speak to her about my family experience with cancer. She and I began to form a bond.

On one occasion, I approached Emy about a situation I dreaded—the possibility of obtaining a doctorate without Mom there to receive it with me. I remember vividly that she proclaimed, "I got my Ph.D. for me and my Mom. She did not see me walk across the stage, but she was there in spirit." I will never forget those words or the lesson she taught me afterward. She explained that, although her mother had passed away, she carried her mom with her at all times. Her mom influenced her personality . . . her perspective on life . . . her essence. She gave this gift to every person she met—a special part of her mom. She made me feel as if I had a wonderful gift to give to everyone too—the personality traits of my parents which had shaped me and influenced my life. I found this concept profound. It was quite different from the "throw yourself into your work" advice and it was a much-needed gift of grace.

One lesson I learned from this administrator was how to release situations with grace. When I joined the program, I was angry and jealous over a breakup with my boyfriend. I knew I needed to let go of the relationship, but that was not enough. Emy taught me to do so with grace—with peace and unconditional acceptance of myself and of others. Initially, I struggled with this idea. Eventually, I understood and applied it. Letting go is the first step in healing. Letting go with grace is a deeper action that allows healing to progress to completion.

Our Program Administrator taught me another important lesson. Once, after seeing me on an autumn Sunday afternoon, she sent

me a note which provided the following phrase: "Look for . . . listen
to . . . gather close . . . the little graces that daily come your way."
This is a simple phrase with a powerful message. On that day, Emy
looked at my smile and at the maple trees, she listened to classical
music and to the crunch of leaves underfoot, and she gathered close
memories of her mother serving Sunday dinner and of her daughter
dancing. This simple phrase and examples she provided are anti-
dotes for distress. She taught me to appreciate graces that come not
only from direct human interactions, which I had enjoyed since join-
ing the program, but also from the everyday sights, sounds, and sen-
sations that make up our lives. I learned that grace surrounds us at all
times; our task is to be open and allow ourselves to receive this gift.

Finally, Emy taught me a plain but important sentiment: Life is
found in human relationships. I often forget this principle when I am
solving equations, designing equipment, or performing rocket science.
Nonetheless, I realize that my relationships with others define me.
Treating others with grace rather than alienation allows one to nurture that which is most important in life—links and interconnections
between human beings.

For the staff, the entire mentoring program was an exercise in
sharing grace with others. Participants were asked to attend
monthly dinner meetings, communicate with their mentoring part-
ners, and complete evaluations. We as staff members encouraged
them to provide support, affirmation, and strategies for success for
each other. We accepted them for who they were rather than for
what they did. When they could not attend a meeting, we welcomed
them without resentment at the next event. When they needed support, we made ourselves available. I found that most participants
were as surprised and delighted to receive grace as I was when I
joined the staff. They were similarly taken aback at the contrast with
the competitive behavior of engineering graduate school.

Unfortunately, I lived in the mentoring program world only a few hours a week. I still spent most of my time competing in engineering. To my way of thinking, the competitive environment bolstered the strong but alienated those perceived to be weak. A regrettable consequence was that my standard behavior and that of some other staff members and participants was to practice alienation. Replacing this with grace was a new activity and required some work.

At each monthly gathering, I practiced looking for, listening to, and gathering close graces. I looked at the abundance of food and at the women enthusiastically eating (once, I remember chocolate-dipped strawberries on display); I listened to the excited chatter during dinner and to the eager participation in icebreakers and discussion topics (once, we listed the things for which we were most thankful—I remember warm discussions of family); I gathered close the empowerment we felt as we dreamed of being like the successful engineers that spoke to us (once, we were riveted as an auto industry executive said her struggles in grad school had all paid off).

As time passed, program participants began to approach me for support when they were being alienated. Once, a doctoral student who was clearly an outgoing leader of others came to me in tears. She said that she was experiencing problems with her advisor and her department chair. She told me that they did not want to write support letters for a fellowship application, allegedly because of her poor performance on the doctoral qualifying exam (although she had passed). It appeared that she was caught in the crossfire of a competition between these two people. Unfortunately, she internalized the situation and felt she was not good enough for the fellowship. I respected her and knew she could win any award for which she applied. I told her how much everyone in the program loved and respected her. I encouraged her to let go of the fellowship opportunity with grace. I urged her to focus instead on pushing ahead and getting her Ph.D.

One of our program goals was to increase the number of women engineering students obtaining graduate degrees in engineering at our university. Our demonstrations of grace toward program participants helped achieve this goal. We provided an environment where they could feel good about themselves regardless of the status of their research or their classes. In turn, they felt better about staying in school and finishing their degrees. Our impact is evident in the following comments we received on surveys:

"I had no idea that we had so many female engineers on campus until I participated in this program."

"Learning about other women in engineering has helped me to see what it takes to be successful."

"Getting to know others that share my feelings made me feel that I am not alone."

My mother became a cancer survivor after thirteen months of treatment. During her recovery, we grew closer as we shared the lessons about grace I had learned in the mentoring program. When she met Emy, they quickly formed a bond of their own. Mom was present at my graduation ceremony and she watched me walk across the stage for my diploma. It was our proudest moment, one made more meaningful because it had almost been taken away.

Years after graduation, I stay in touch with many mentoring program staff members and participants. I watch them achieve success at companies, laboratories, and universities around the world. The women I helped through stressful times are my most loyal friends. Looking back, I gave them a special gift that Emy had given me. I shared a little part of her personality—the part filled with grace—with them.

Now I actively seek relationships with other women to counter the alienation I often feel in a male-dominated field. One networking group I belong to consists of about ten women employed in different professions. They are social workers, accountants, criminal investigators, and business managers, to name a few. We go away for a weekend each year, and we support each other throughout the year with phone calls, emails, and social gatherings.

Perhaps the most significant outcome of the lessons I learned at Purdue was my preparation to enter a healthy romantic relationship. Shortly after graduation, I began to date the man I would eventually marry. As a result of my growth, I was ready to receive his kindness and to grace him with my own. While my prior relationships were based on insecurity, this one was anchored in mutual respect and support. This man has been my husband for almost a year.

After graduation, I had other difficult encounters. The prestigious institute where I worked was competitive. I felt that my supervisor focused on what I could not do rather than what I accomplished. I tried to talk with him about my need for support and affirmation. I sensed he did not understand me, and my efforts at communication only made things worse. I was alienated and in need of grace. I remembered another lesson from Emy: You cannot change others. You can only change yourself in relationship to others. I worked on myself. I began to accept my supervisor as he was. This was hard work, but I persisted for several years. I knew I needed to find my supporters. By grace, they found me. Some powerful people began to trumpet my success. Their gestures countered my alienation.

In time, I realized that I should allow myself some grace. I knew I could not single-handedly change my workplace. Instead, I focused on something I had the power to change: I looked for a new job. It was hard to let go of the idea of a career with that first, prestigious organization, but I worked to do so with grace. To my delight, I was offered a research job at another prestigious organization. My senior scientist friends had written strong letters of recommendation for me. I had changed the things I could while releasing—with grace—those I could not.

When I started my first job, I was awe-struck by one of the famous scientists within the institute. His research results appeared in prominent textbooks in our field. Yet, during midlife and at the height of his career, he had retired. During his weekly visits to the office, we would sometimes engage in deep discussions about the current state of science. Once, he said his contributions to our field were not appreciated. He felt his work would ultimately be forgotten. Upon further discussion, it became clear to me that although he was respected outside the walls of our institute, he had been alienated for years by his own managers. As this luminary questioned himself, I began to tell him stories. I told him students were reading his papers in droves and hoping to be like him. I told him he was special to me and to others. His face softened as he received this grace.

Postdoctoral fellows (post-docs) are vulnerable because their positions are temporary and they are just beginning their careers. Perhaps the most creative person I have met was a post-doc at my first job. His mind raced with innovative ideas, and he worked hard. Yet during his appraisal, he received a poor rating. He was told that post-docs were ineligible for raises. This was incorrect; other post-docs got nice raises that year. He took his concerns to higher managers but was discounted. I repeatedly told him (as I had for months) how contagious his energy and enthusiasm for life were to those around him. I urged him to let go of the pain and to look forward to bigger, better things in his future. Grace flowed through me to him that day.

There is a little book on my desk that offers practical advice and strategies to those about to embark on a scientific career. My business card is stapled to its inside cover. I give the little book to almost every new researcher that visits my office. I tell them to take it home and return it after it is read. I usually get a note of thanks when the book comes back. I occasionally chuckle when I look at that book on my desk because it has traveled extensively. This little book is a gift I give which delivers grace to me a few weeks later.

Others have appreciated the grace I have passed along. When I left my first job, my coworkers held a farewell luncheon for me. I was touched by several speeches that were delivered. My colleagues shared their delight at my ability to connect with people, my community volunteer work, and my communication skills. I was surprised but thankful to hear my colleagues openly discuss what many of them feel are "soft" topics.

The network of people I have helped rewards me in tangible ways. I recently called a former post-doc for help on a research problem. He dropped everything to remind me of some basic principles it would have taken me hours to find in textbooks. In another case, a former post-doc who is now a professor recommended that I hire one of her students as an intern. I hired him and he has made a phenomenal contribution. Additionally, those who have studied my little book are appreciative. They approach me at conferences with familiarity. They are just beginning careers; I expect they will be gracing me for the rest of mine.

I have found a job that I really enjoy. My manager is supportive and does not practice alienation. Within the first year, I have been given responsibilities that would have been reserved for veterans at my first job. I am thankful for the grace of a new workplace.

One of the first things I did in my current job was sign up for the mentoring program. I have lunch with my mentor every other week, and we regularly attend company-sponsored mentoring sessions. We have become quite close. With her, I feel grace through connection. I never would have joined this program if I had not learned about grace and mentoring at Purdue.

As I approach the five-year anniversary of defending my dissertation, I reflect and realize how much I have learned about the value of giving and receiving grace during times of alienation.

In graduate school, each of us suffered from being on the wrong side of an imbalance of power. The closer we got to graduation, the more we wanted our degrees. The more we wanted those diplomas, the more vulnerable we were to alienation by those in power. We were primed to learn about grace.

In earning our advanced degrees, we would eventually obtain power of our own. The lessons we learned about countering alienation with grace are useful for anyone striving to achieve a goal in a competitive environment. As you work to obtain power of your own, look for, listen to, and gather close your daily gifts. Attenuate the negative messages you hear while amplifying the positive ones. Accept yourself and accept others.

Most importantly, promise yourself that when you finally obtain power of your own, you will use it in a kinder and more compassionate way. Refrain from alienating people. Experience grace and share grace and create environments full of grace for others. Love people for who they are rather than what they do. If each of us approaches our career and life in this way, people will suffer less. We owe this to each other. After all, life is in human relationships.

LINDA G. BLEVINS has received three degrees in Mechanical Engineering, a BS from the University of Alabama in 1989, an MS from Virginia Tech in 1992, and a PhD from Purdue University in 1996. She then took a position as a research staff member at the National Institute of Standards and Technology. In the year 2000 she was married to Greg Fiechtner who also has a PhD in Mechanical Engineering from Purdue. The two of them have moved to the West Coast where they are researchers for Sandia National Laboratories in Livermore, California.

Outcomes

This book has been a process by which a group of individuals have shared encounters, gained insights, raised awareness, integrated thoughts, and constructed meaning out of their lives. Hopefully, the reader can sense their reverence for life, respect for people, appreciation for human relationships, along with their compassionate and caring spirits. These people cherish and nurture their friendships. They have replenished each other through interconnected actions and have passed their experiences on to others.

This book includes 12 paired actions which themselves can be linked together. *Welcoming,* being receptive to others, relates to *communicating,* listening to others, which can lead to *trusting,* relying on others, which has to do with *accepting,* appreciating others, and *affirming,* praising others. Continuing, *forgiving,* overlooking mistakes, relates to *reframing,* perceiving one can make mistakes, which can lead to *letting go* of one's fear of making mistakes. Further, *rejoicing,* honoring special events, relates to *balancing,* having leisure time, which has to do with *focusing* at quiet moments and *gracing,* appreciating unexpected gifts.

We realize that paired actions in life, such as accepting/rejecting or rejoicing/grieving, will contribute to our development. For example, approval of others, accepting, could stem from a series of stinging slights, rejecting. Great delight, rejoicing, can come from experiencing deep sorrow, grieving. Together polarities do exist and paired actions can be rival elements battling within our inner selves. The challenge is to make actions work for us, setting us up for success rather than failure over time.

Contributors to this book have noted that they learned the importance of:

- reaching out and welcoming others,
- listening to and communicating with others,
- being a reliable person,
- accepting and appreciating differences in people,
- encouraging ownership and commitment in people,
- growing from one's mistakes,
- reframing situations in life,
- allowing others to see your real self,
- capturing and relishing joy,
- balancing conflicting demands in our lives,
- enabling ourselves to focus, reflect, and regroup, and
- giving and receiving grace.

After reading their stories I realized that we have mentored one another. My ideas and actions have guided and impacted their lives. In turn, their thoughts and behaviors have enriched and affected my life. I have nurtured them, yet they have nurtured me. Really, what we have given to each another has come back to us in fuller measure. We have renewed, replenished, reformed, and reestablished ourselves. Our lives have been and continue to be interwoven, linked together through our actions and relationships. Together we have survived and will continue to survive crises. We have brought each other to fuller growth as human beings.

Now, after reflecting on the decade that I spent administering mentoring programs, I can distinguish positive movement. I comprehend how personal struggles have become connected with professional endeavors. How fragments have become united over time to allow a sense of peace to enrich my existence. How life has moved from the particular to the universal. How my own growth, understanding, unification, joy in being me have been transmitted to students. Then how they in turn, with renewed courage and energy, have passed their development on to others. *Together we have discovered how to nurture human relationships through giving much, and in the process we are receiving back or gaining more.*

—Emily M. Wadsworth

About the Author

EMILY M. WADSWORTH grew up in Ithaca, New York. She earned a BFA degree at Cornell University, an MS degree at Oregon State University, and a PhD degree at Purdue University. She was the creator and administrator, from 1991–1999, for both the Undergraduate and Graduate Mentoring Programs for females in the Schools of Engineering at Purdue. The programs were recognized in 1997 with a Presidential Award for Excellence in Engineering Mentoring from President William Clinton at the White House. This award was, and is, administered by the National Science Foundation. She has been married to Dr. Henry A. Wadsworth for 47 years. They are now retired and live in West Lafayette, Indiana.